As an appreciation for your purchase, we want to offer you the FREE BLW Essential Toolkit for you to enjoy.

*To get access, simply scan the QR code or go to:*

*(If you prefer, email us at info@infantnook.com)*

In this kit you will find:

- ◎ BLW Practical Nutrition Charts to ensure a balanced diet.
- ◎ Food and Adverse Reaction Log to monitor your baby's progress.
- ◎ Additional tips to simplify and optimize your BLW experience.

If you want to feel more confident and secure on your complementary feeding journey, don't forget to download this valuable gift. Your baby deserves it!

# CONTENTS

**My Journey with Baby-Led Weaning**

# PART I: THE FUNDAMENTALS OF BABY-LED WEANING

- Definition and key principles
- BLW vs. traditional complementary feeding: what's the difference?
- The proven benefits of BLW for babies and families

- Developmental signs that indicate your baby is prepared
- The importance of posture and coordination
- Demystifying the extrusion reflex and other milestones

- Useful accessories and safety considerations
- Adapting the feeding space for success
- Fostering a positive family atmosphere around food

# PART II: STARTING THE BLW ADVENTURE

- ◎ Nutrient-dense and easy-to-grip foods
- ◎ The crucial role of iron and how to ensure it
- ◎ Daily protein quantity according to food types
- ◎ How many meals per day should I offer my baby?
- ◎ Plate method

- ◎ Guide to appropriate sizes and shapes for each stage
- ◎ Progressing from soft to firmer and more challenging
- ◎ Tips for adapting family foods to BLW

- ◎ Introduction of major allergens: latest recommendations
- ◎ Identifying and responding to allergic reactions
- ◎ BLW for babies with known allergies or intolerances

# PART III: OVERCOMING COMMON BLW CHALLENGES

- ◎ Understanding the difference between gagging and choking
- ◎ Key first aid techniques for safe feeding
- ◎ Strategies for managing parental anxiety
- ◎ Foods that require special attention

# BLW:
## YOUR ESSENTIAL GUIDE
## TO SMART
## BABY-LED
## WEANING

### YOUR BABY'S FIRST BITES
A PRACTICAL HANDBOOK FOR HEALTHY
COMPLEMENTARY FEEDING FOR COMMITTED PARENTS

## INFANT NOOK

INCLUDES
RECIPES

# Infant Nook

Every word has been written from the heart.

If this book has been useful to you and you want to help me, write an honest opinion. I promise you it will only take a few seconds, and it will make a big difference to me.

**Thank you, thank you, a thousand thanks!**

# INTRODUCTION

## My Journey with Baby-Led Weaning

*Dear mother or father,*

If you are reading these lines, it is very likely that you find yourself at a crucial and transformative moment in your life: the introduction of solid foods into your little one's diet. As a mother and expert in infant feeding, I know firsthand that this process can generate a mixture of excitement, doubts, and concerns.

When my first child was about to turn six months old, I felt overwhelmed by the amount of conflicting information on when and how to start with solids. It was then that I discovered Baby-Led Weaning (BLW), an approach that resonated deeply with my values and vision of respectful parenting centered on the individual needs of the baby.

As I delved into the scientific research and began to apply the BLW principles with my own son, I marveled at the results. Not only was he enjoying a wide variety of foods autonomously and safely, but I could also see how this experience strengthened our bond, fostered his integral development, and laid the foundations for a healthy long-term relationship with food. Fueled by my own transformative experience, I decided to delve even deeper into this fascinating field and dedicate my career to helping other families discover the benefits of BLW. Over the years, I have encountered many families who, despite being attracted to BLW, feel overwhelmed by the lack of clear and reliable information.

That is why I decided to write this book: to offer you a comprehensive guide, based on scientific evidence and practical experience, that will accompany you at every step of your BLW journey. My aim is to empower you to trust your own instinct and your baby's innate wisdom, providing you with the necessary tools and support to fully enjoy this exciting stage. Throughout these pages, I will share with you not only the theoretical foundations of BLW, but also practical tips, menu ideas, strategies to face common challenges and, most importantly, an encouraging and compassionate perspective that understands the realities of modern parenting. This book will guide you from the basic principles of BLW to the most advanced considerations, addressing topics such as baby readiness, food selection, allergy management, overcoming choking fears, and much more. All supported by the latest scientific research.

But beyond the practical information, my desire is to invite you to see complementary feeding as a unique opportunity to nourish not only the body, but also the mind and spirit of your baby. BLW is much more than a method of introducing solids; it is a philosophy that promotes autonomy, confidence, and pleasure in eating from the earliest infancy. So, I encourage you to embark on this adventure with curiosity, patience and, above all, with the certainty that you are offering your child the best possible start in their relationship with food. Trust the process, celebrate each small achievement, and enjoy the wonderful experience of watching your baby flourish before your eyes. With all my love and admiration for the important work you do.

*Amelia Benet*

# PART I:

# THE FUNDAMENTALS OF BABY-LED WEANING

# Chapter 1: What is Baby-Led Weaning?

*"Let food be thy medicine and medicine be thy food."* -
*Hippocrates*

Imagine for a moment your little one sitting in their high chair, with a sparkle of curiosity in their eyes as they observe the colorful plate of food in front of them. Instead of passively waiting to be fed spoonful by spoonful, your baby extends their chubby little hand, grabs a piece of steamed broccoli, and brings it to their mouth with determination. They chew with concentration, exploring the soft texture and slightly bitter flavor, and then flash a satisfied smile before reaching for the next bite.

This scene, as natural as it is extraordinary, is the very essence of Baby-Led Weaning (BLW) or self-directed complementary feeding. Unlike traditional methods of introducing solids, where parents control the process by feeding the baby purees and porridges, BLW invites the little one to take the reins of their own food learning from the start. In BLW, the baby is encouraged to explore and experiment with whole, soft foods, cut into pieces or sticks the size of their little fist, which they can easily grasp and bring to their mouth on their own. There are no spoons, no airplanes buzzing towards the baby's mouth, no struggle to get them to eat "just one more spoonful". Instead, the baby's pace, preferences, and satiety cues are respected, trusting their innate ability to self-regulate their intake and develop feeding skills naturally and progressively.

But BLW is much more than simply "letting the baby feed themselves". It is a holistic philosophy that recognizes the baby as a competent and active being in their own development, and promotes their autonomy, self-confidence, and full participation in the sensory and social experience of family meals. It is important to note that during the first 12 months, breast milk or formula should continue to be the main source of nutrition for your baby. The AAP recommends breastfeeding as the sole source of nutrition for your baby for about 6 months. When you add solid foods to your baby's diet, continue breastfeeding until at least 12 months. BLW is a form of complementary feeding that does not replace breastfeeding, but rather complements it, allowing your baby to explore new flavors, textures, and skills at their own pace.

**The key principles underlying BLW include:**

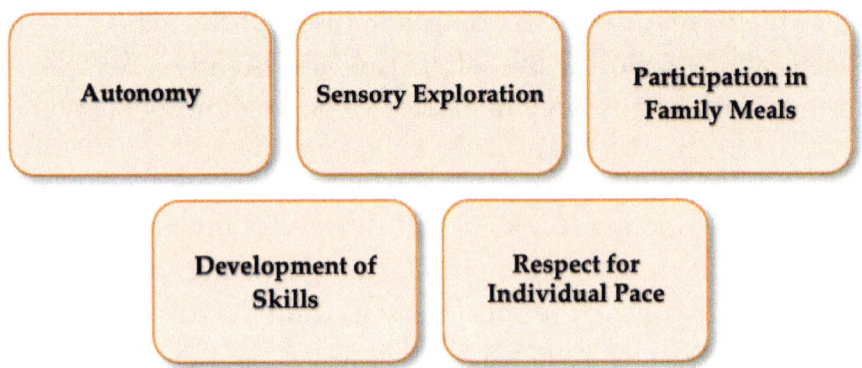

1. **Autonomy**: The baby decides what to eat, how much to eat, and at what pace, based on their own internal cues of hunger and satiety. They are not forced to eat more than they want, nor are they restricted access to certain foods. They are trusted in their innate ability to choose a balanced and varied diet, as long as they are offered healthy and age-appropriate options.

2. **Sensory Exploration**: The baby is encouraged to explore food with all their senses, including touch, smell, and sight, in addition to taste. Touching, smelling, looking at, manipulating, and even playing with food is considered an essential part of the learning process. Through this multisensory exploration, the baby develops fine motor skills, hand-eye coordination, awareness of textures and temperatures, and a more positive and curious relationship with food.

3. **Participation in Family Meals**: From the beginning, the baby is invited to sit at the table with the rest of the family, to share the same foods (with necessary adaptations), and to participate in the conversation and social interaction typical of meals. This fosters their sense of belonging, their capacity for imitation and learning by example, and their enjoyment of food as a shared and pleasurable experience.

4. **Development of Skills**: BLW encourages the development of fine motor skills, hand-eye coordination, and the oral skills necessary for independent feeding.

5. **Respect for Individual Pace**: Each baby is unique and allowed to progress in complementary feeding at their own pace, without external pressures. In BLW there is no strict calendar of food introduction or an "ideal" amount that the baby should eat at each stage. Their curiosity, appetite, and willingness to try new flavors and textures are respected, without rigid pressures or expectations. If one day the baby eats very little or rejects a certain food, they are not forced or seen as a problem. They are trusted to, with patience and repeated exposure, expand their range of acceptance.

### BLW vs. Traditional Complementary Feeding: What's the Difference?

Unlike BLW, traditional methods of complementary feeding are usually based on the gradual introduction of purees and porridges, with parents or caregivers controlling what, when, and how much the baby eats.

| Aspect | BLW | Traditional feeding |
|---|---|---|
| Control of feeding | The baby decides what and how much to eat | Parents control portions and pace |
| Texture of foods | Soft pieces and appropriately sized for grasping | Smooth purees and porridges |
| Family meal participation | Baby eats same foods as family | Special meals prepared for the baby |
| Skill development | Autonomy and fine motor skills fostered | Nutrient intake prioritized over exploration |
| Relationship with food | Intuitive and healthy relationship promoted | Higher risk of overfeeding or power struggles |

It is important to note that BLW is not an "all or nothing" approach; many families opt for a combined method, incorporating some BLW principles while also offering purees or foods specially prepared for the baby. The most important thing is to find the balance that works best for your family and your individual baby.

## The Proven Benefits of BLW for Babies and Families

More and more studies support the multiple benefits of Baby-Led Weaning for the development and well-being of babies, as well as for overall family dynamics. Some of the key benefits include:

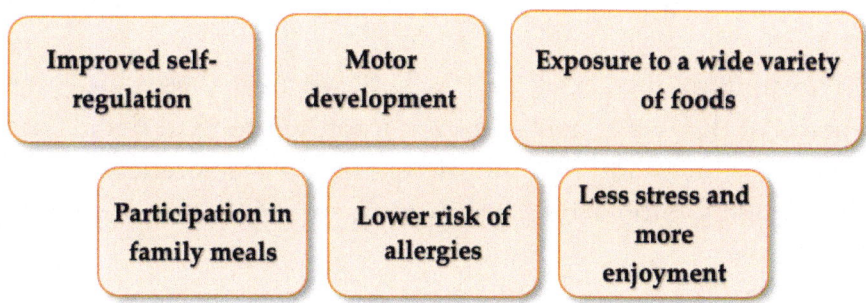

1. **Improved self-regulation:** Babies who follow BLW tend to be better at self-regulating their food intake according to their individual needs, which may reduce the risk of overfeeding and long-term obesity.

2. **Motor development:** The practice of grasping, manipulating, and bringing food to the mouth encourages the development of fine motor skills and hand-eye coordination

3. **Exposure to a wide variety of foods:** BLW allows babies to explore a broader range of textures, flavors, and nutrients from the start, which can lead to heathier and more diverse food preferences.

4. **Participation in family meals:** By eating the same foods as the rest of the family, babies feel included and learn by imitation, fostering social skills and a sense of belonging.

5. **Lower risk of allergies:** Some studies *(Perkin et al., 2016; Nwaru et al., 2014)* suggest that early introduction of allergenic foods through BLW may reduce the risk of developing food allergies.

6. **Less stress and more enjoyment:** BLW meals tend to be more relaxed and enjoyable for everyone, as the baby's natural pace is respected and exploration and discovery are encouraged.

Throughout this book, we will delve into these and other benefits of BLW. But before diving into the practical details, it is crucial to understand that the success of BLW is not measured by how much food the baby ingests or how perfectly they handle the food pieces.

As mothers and fathers, our role is to provide a safe and enriching environment for our baby to explore food at their own pace, offering healthy and age-appropriate options.

# Key points of the chapter

o *BLW is a baby-led approach to complementary feeding, based on trust in their innate abilities to self-regulate intake and develop skills.*

o *It differs from traditional methods in aspects such as control of feeding, food texture, and participation in family meals.*

o *Proven benefits include improved self-regulation, motor development, exposure to a wide variety of foods, lower risk of allergies, and greater enjoyment of meals.*

o *The success of BLW is measured by fostering a healthy and positive relationship with food, rather than the quantity ingested or the perfection in handling foods.*

# Chapter 2: Is Your Baby Ready for BLW?

*"The future belongs to those who believe in the beauty of their dreams." - Eleanor Roosevelt*

Imagine for a moment that you are preparing dinner while your baby watches you from their high chair. Suddenly, you notice that their gaze is fixed on the mango you are cutting, and their little hand reaches out towards the fruit with evident interest. "Do you want to try it?" you ask with a smile, and bring a small piece to their hand. With surprising dexterity, your baby grabs the mango, brings it to their mouth, and starts nibbling on it with delight, leaving you astonished and a bit confused. "Aren't they supposed to be too young for solid foods?" you wonder.

If you have experienced a similar scene or simply feel curious about knowing when and how to start with complementary feeding, you may be wondering if your baby is ready for BLW. The answer, like so many other things in parenting, is that each child is unique and develops at their own pace. There is no magic age or rigid list of requirements to start with BLW. However, there are certain developmental signs that may indicate that your baby is physically and psychologically mature to explore solid foods autonomously.

## Developmental Signs that Indicate Your Baby is Prepared

Each baby is unique and will reach developmental milestones at their own pace. However, there are certain signs that usually appear around 6 months of age and suggest that your baby is mature enough to start with BLW.

These signs include:

| | | |
|---|---|---|
| Sitting with little or no assistance | Good head and neck control | Hand-eye-mouth coordination |
| Interest in food | Disappearance of the extrusion reflex | |

1. **Sitting with little or no assistance:** Your baby should be able to maintain an upright and stable posture while seated, either on your lap or in a high chair. This ability will allow them to have their hands free to safely explore and manipulate food.

2. **Good head and neck control**: Your baby should have sufficient strength and stability in the head and neck to maintain an upright position and move the head from side to side with ease.

3. **Hand-eye-mouth coordination**: Observe if your baby can look at an object, accurately reach for it, grasp it firmly, and bring it to their mouth deliberately. This coordination is essential for self-feeding.

4. **Interest in food**: Does your baby curiously observe when you eat, try to reach for your plate, or open their mouth when you bring food close to them? These are clear signs that they are developing a genuine interest in food and are eager to participate in family meals.

5. **Disappearance of the extrusion reflex**: Around 4-6 months, the extrusion reflex (when the baby automatically sticks out their tongue when feeling something on their lips) begins to diminish, allowing the baby to move food to the back of the mouth for swallowing.

It is important to keep in mind that your baby does not need to show all these signs simultaneously to start with BLW. Each little one develops at a different pace, and some may be ready to explore solid foods a little before or after 6 months. The crucial thing is to observe your baby and respond to their individual signs of readiness. It is not about rushing the process or comparing them to other children, but rather waiting for your baby to show you that they are physically and psychologically prepared to take this step.

## The Importance of Posture and Coordination

Of all the developmental signs mentioned, the ability to sit unsupported and hand-eye-mouth coordination are particularly important to ensure a safe and successful experience with BLW.

When your baby can sit stably, either on your lap or in a high chair, they have a solid base to explore food with confidence. An upright posture also facilitates digestion and reduces the risk of choking, as it allows food to move more naturally from the mouth to the stomach.

Hand-eye-mouth coordination, on the other hand, is fundamental for your baby to self-feed effectively. At first, your little one may have difficulty grasping foods or bringing them to their mouth accurately, but with practice, these skills will be perfected. Your role is to provide foods of appropriate size and texture, and give your baby ample opportunity to practice these skills.

If your baby cannot yet sit unsupported or has difficulty coordinating their movements, don't worry. You can start offering soft and easy-to-grasp foods while holding them on your lap or supporting them with pillows in a high chair. As their strength and coordination improve, they will be able to take on a more independent role at mealtimes.

## Demystifying the Extrusion Reflex and Other Milestones

One of the most common misconceptions about BLW is that babies cannot start with solid foods until they have completely lost the extrusion reflex. While it is true that this reflex can make it difficult for the baby to move food to the back of the mouth for swallowing, it is not necessary to wait for it to disappear completely before offering solid foods. *(Martínez Rubio et al., 2021; American Academy of Pediatrics, 2023)*

In fact, practice with soft foods and small pieces can help the baby learn to manage food in their mouth and gradually overcome the extrusion reflex. As your baby experiences different textures and learns to chew and swallow, this reflex will naturally integrate into their development of feeding skills.

Another milestone that often worries mothers and fathers is the appearance of teeth. Many believe that babies need to have teeth to start with BLW, but this is not true. A baby's gums are surprisingly strong and capable of chewing soft foods, and the action of biting and chewing itself can alleviate teething discomfort. Of course, when teeth do appear, your baby will be able to handle a wider variety of textures and firmer foods. But there is no need to delay the start of BLW until they have a complete set of teeth.

# Key points of the chapter

o   *Developmental signs that indicate a baby may be ready for BLW include: sitting unsupported, good head and neck control, hand-eye-mouth coordination, interest in food, and diminished extrusion reflex.*

o   *Stable posture and coordination are especially important for a safe and successful experience with BLW.*

o   *It is not necessary to wait for the extrusion reflex to disappear completely or for the baby to have teeth to start with BLW.*

o   *Each baby develops at their own pace, and the most important thing is to observe and respond to their individual signs of readiness*

.

# Chapter 3: Creating a Safe and Conducive Environment for BLW

*"Preparation is the key to success."* - *Alexander Graham Bel*

Continuing with the visualization of the scenes that will soon become everyday, now I want you to imagine for a moment the scenario of a safe and conducive environment: a baby sitting comfortably in their high chair, with a wide variety of healthy and appetizing foods within reach of their hand. Around them, a smiling and relaxed family, sharing anecdotes and laughter while enjoying the same dishes. The little one explores the different textures and flavors with enthusiasm, getting their face and hands dirty without anyone being alarmed by it. From time to time, they offer them a new food or bring them a glass of water, but always respecting their pace and satiety cues. At the end of the meal, the little one babbles with satisfaction and the family clears the table naturally, celebrating the small achievements of the day.

It sounds idyllic, doesn't it? Well, although it may seem like a scene out of a commercial, I assure you that it is a realistic and achievable goal for any family that sets out to create a safe and conducive environment for BLW. Because beyond the baby's skills or the type of food offered, the physical and emotional environment in which meals take place is a key factor for the success and enjoyment of BLW.

## Useful Accessories and Safety Considerations

While BLW does not require specialized equipment, there are some elements that can make the process safer, easier, and less messy. Some useful items include:

1. **Safe high chair or baby seat**: Choose a stable high chair with an easy-to-clean tray or surface, and make sure your baby is always supervised and properly secured. We want it to allow your little one to sit upright and stable, with their feet supported and their back straight.

2. **Long-sleeved bibs**: Bibs with sleeves can help protect your baby's clothing during meals, especially in the early stages of BLW when messes are common.

3. **Easy-to-clean tablecloth or mat**: Placing a tablecloth or mat under your baby's high chair can make cleanup easier after meals.

4. **Baby-safe plates and utensils:** Opt for unbreakable plates and cups with non-slip bases, and soft, easy-to-grasp plastic or silicone utensils for when your baby starts showing interest in using them. Pre-spoons, with a thick handle and a flat, shallow bowl, are ideal for the early stages.

In addition to equipment, some safety considerations are crucial when practicing BLW:

1. **Constant supervision**: Always supervise your baby during meals and never leave them alone while eating, even for a brief moment.

2. **Food size and shape**: Offer soft foods cut into finger-sized pieces or large enough for your baby to grasp and chew safely, avoiding hard, small, or round foods that may pose a choking hazard.

3. **Distraction-free environment**: Minimize distractions during meals, such as television or toys, so that your baby can focus on eating and you can be attentive to any signs of difficulty.

4. **First aid skills**: Familiarize yourself with infant first aid techniques, including what to do in case of choking.

## Adapting the Feeding Space for Success

In addition to having the proper equipment and following safety guidelines, it is important to create a feeding space that promotes BLW success and enjoyment. Here are some tips:

1. **Choose a comfortable location**: Make sure your baby's highchair or seat is in a comfortable place for you and them, preferably near the family table so they feel included in meals.

| Tray/table above chest, elbows low | Full mobility. Elbows above tray. Easily reaches food |
|---|---|

2. **Adequate lighting**: Make sure the feeding area has good lighting so you can clearly see your baby and be alert to any signs of difficulty.

3. **Easy access to food**: Place foods within your baby's reach so they can explore and grasp them on their own. You can use plates or trays with compartments to separate different types of food.

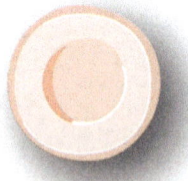 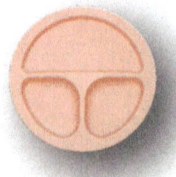 

4. **Keep things simple**: It is not necessary to have a wide variety of utensils or accessories. Focus on providing nutritious and age-appropriate foods, and let your baby explore and learn at their own pace.

5. **Allow for messes**: Accept that messes are a normal part of the learning process. Place a mat or tablecloth under the high chair to facilitate cleaning and have wet wipes or a cloth handy to clean your baby after meals.

## Fostering a Positive Family Atmosphere Around Food

BLW is not just about the mechanics of feeding, but also about fostering a positive and relaxed atmosphere around meals. Some tips for creating an enjoyable experience for all family members include:

1. **Eating together as a family**: Whenever possible, sit down to eat with your baby. This not only provides a role model, but also turns meals into a time of connection and social learning.

2. **Offering a variety of healthy foods**: Provide a selection of nutritious foods at each meal, including different colors, textures, and food groups. This exposes your baby to a wide range of flavors and nutrients, and allows them to explore their own preferences.

3. **Letting the baby set the pace**: Let your baby decide how much to eat and at what speed. Avoid pressuring them to eat more or trying to rush the process. Trust your baby's innate ability to self-regulate and know when they are finished.

4. **Staying relaxed about messes**: Accept that messes are a normal and necessary part of the learning process. Instead of stressing about cleaning, enjoy watching your baby explore and experiment with food.

5. **Praising the process, not the results**: Focus on your baby's learning and exploration process, rather than on how much food they consume. Praise your baby for trying new foods, skillfully manipulating foods, and participating in family meals.

In essence, proper preparation is key to a successful and safe BLW experience. By recognizing your baby's signs of readiness, having the necessary equipment and safety precautions, and fostering a positive mealtime environment, you can set the stage for a rewarding and enriching complementary feeding journey.

## Key points

o *Useful accessories for BLW include a safe high chair, long-sleeved bibs, easy-to-clean tablecloths, and baby-friendly plates and utensils.*

o *Key safety considerations are constant supervision, offering soft and appropriately sized foods, minimizing distractions, and knowing first aid techniques.*

o *Adapting the feeding space with adequate lighting, easy access to food, and accepting messes can promote BLW success.*

o *Foster a positive atmosphere in family meals by offering a variety of healthy foods, allowing the baby to set the pace, and focusing on the learning process rather than the quantity consumed.*

# PART II:

# STARTING THE BLW ADVENTURE

# Chapter 4: First Foods: Where to Start?

*"Simplicity is the ultimate sophistication." - Leonardo da Vinci*

The long-awaited moment has arrived! Your baby is showing all the signs of being ready to start with solid foods and you have prepared the perfect environment for a safe and successful BLW experience. But where to begin? What foods are most suitable for a 6-month-old baby? How do I know if a food is soft and safe enough? Do I have to cook special meals for my baby or can I adapt what the rest of the family eats? Don't worry, it's normal to feel a bit overwhelmed at first!

In this chapter, we will explore what foods are most suitable for the first BLW attempts, the crucial role of iron in your baby's diet, and some menu ideas for the first weeks.

## Nutrient-Rich and Easy-to-Grip Foods

When it comes to the first foods to offer in BLW, it is essential to choose nutritious and varied options, including the different food groups, and they must be safe and easy for your baby to manipulate.

# Food Groups and Frequency of Consumption

| Food Group | Daily Frequency |
|---|---|
| Fruits | 2-3 portions |
| Vegetables | 2-3 portions |
| Proteins | 1-2 portions |
| Grains and Tubers | 2-3 portions |
| Dairy | 1-2 portions |
| Healthy Fats | 1-2 portions |

Therefore, it is important to offer your baby a wide variety of fruits and vegetables from the beginning. This not only ensures an adequate intake of vitamins, minerals, and fiber, but also allows them to explore different flavors and textures, laying the foundation for healthy food preferences in the long term.

To maximize nutritional and economic benefits, try to choose seasonal fruits and vegetables whenever possible. These foods tend to be fresher, tastier, and more affordable than those produced out of season or coming from afar. In addition, opting for local and seasonal products is a way to support farmers in your area and reduce the environmental impact associated with long-distance food transportation.

## Seasonal Fruits and Vegetables Chart

| Season | Fruits | Vegetables |
|---|---|---|
| Spring | Strawberries, cherries, apricots, nectarines | Asparagus, peas, broad beans, spinach, chard, artichokes |
| Summer | Melon, watermelon, figs, plums, peaches, grapes | Tomatoes, eggplant, zucchini, peppers, cucumbers, corn |
| Autumn | Apples, pears, quinces, pomegranates, persimmons | Pumpkin, sweet potatoes, mushrooms, leeks, Brussels sprouts, cauliflower, broccoli |
| Winter | Oranges, tangerines, grapefruits, kiwis, bananas | Carrots, potatoes, onions, celery, turnips, beets, cabbage, lettuce |

Remember that this is just a general guide and the availability of fruits and vegetables may vary depending on your geographic location and weather conditions. By choosing seasonal produce, you will not only be offering your baby the highest quality foods, but also teaching them to appreciate the diversity and natural rhythms of food.

The American Academy of Pediatrics (AAP) recommend starting with foods rich in iron and zinc, as well as those that are common in the family diet and which you feel comfortable offering.

## The Crucial Role of Iron and How to Ensure It

Iron is an essential nutrient for your baby's healthy development, especially for their growth, cognitive development, and immune function. Around 6 months, the iron stores your baby accumulated during pregnancy begin to diminish, so it is crucial to include iron sources in their complementary feeding diet.

### There are two types of iron in food

| Heme Iron | Non-Heme Iron |
|---|---|
| Foods of animal origin | Foods of plant origin |
| Red meat, poultry and fish | Legumes, green leafy vegetables, and fortified cereals |
| Easier for the body to absorb | Less bioavailable and requires certain factors to improve its absorption |

## Foods that are high in iron (100 mg)

| Clams, cockles, mussels 25 mg | Quinoa 13 mg | Sesame seeds 10 mg | Wheat bran, millet 8 - 11 mg | Soy 8.5 mg |
|---|---|---|---|---|
| Mussels 7 mg | Pistachios 7mg | Chickpeas, broad beans, lentils 6 - 8 mg | Peanuts, walnuts, almonds 4 - 5 mg | Oat 4.7mg |
| Anchovies 4.6 mg | Spinach 3 mg | Red meat 3 - 4 mg | Egg yolk 2.7 mg | Pork, chicken, turkey, sea bass 1 - 2 mg |

## Factors that enhance iron absorption

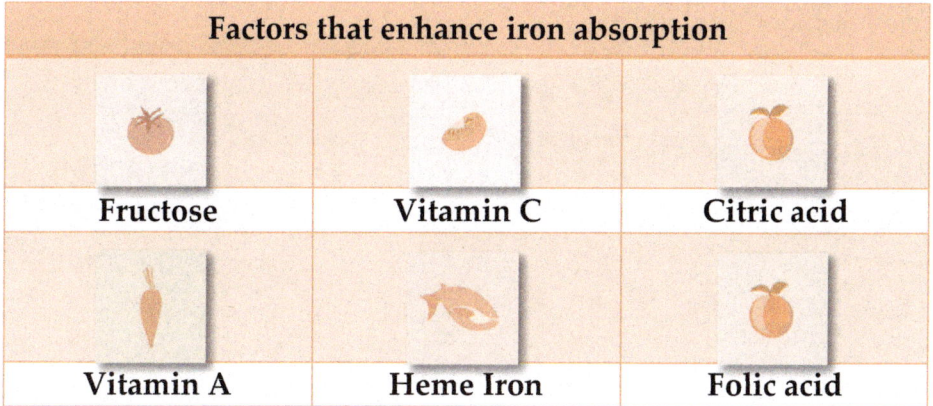

| Fructose | Vitamin C | Citric acid |
|---|---|---|
| Vitamin A | Heme Iron | Folic acid |

## Factors that enhance iron absorption

o **Vitamin C**: Combine iron-rich foods with vitamin C sources, such as citrus fruits (orange, lemon), peppers, kiwi or broccoli.

o **Animal proteins**: The presence of meat, fish or poultry in the same meal can increase iron absorption from other foods.

## Factors that inhibit iron absorption

o **Phytates**: Present in whole grains, legumes and seeds. Soaking, sprouting or fermenting these foods can reduce the phytate content.

o **Calcium**: Although an essential nutrient, calcium can inhibit iron absorption if consumed in large amounts in the same meal.

To make sure your baby is getting enough iron, try to include an iron-rich source at each main meal. If you are concerned that your baby is not getting enough, talk to your pediatrician about the possibility of iron supplements and request a check of their levels.

Remember that symptoms of iron deficiency can be subtle, but include paleness, fatigue, irritability, lack of appetite, and developmental delay.

| Symptoms of low iron | | | | |
|---|---|---|---|---|
| Asymptomatic | Tiredness | Anorexia | Growth alterations | Decreased defenses |
| Paleness | Sleep alteration | Psychomotor development alterations | Lack of hair, fine and sparse | Cold hands and feet |

Premature babies, low-birth-weight babies, twins, and babies born to mothers with anemia have a higher risk of developing iron deficiency, so it is especially important to monitor their intake and levels. *(Anales de Pediatría. 2011).*

## Daily Protein Quantity according to Food Types

In addition to iron, proteins are another fundamental nutrient for the optimal growth and development of your baby.

Keep in mind that more is not always better when it comes to protein. Excessive consumption can overload the baby's immature kidneys and increase the risk of long-term obesity.

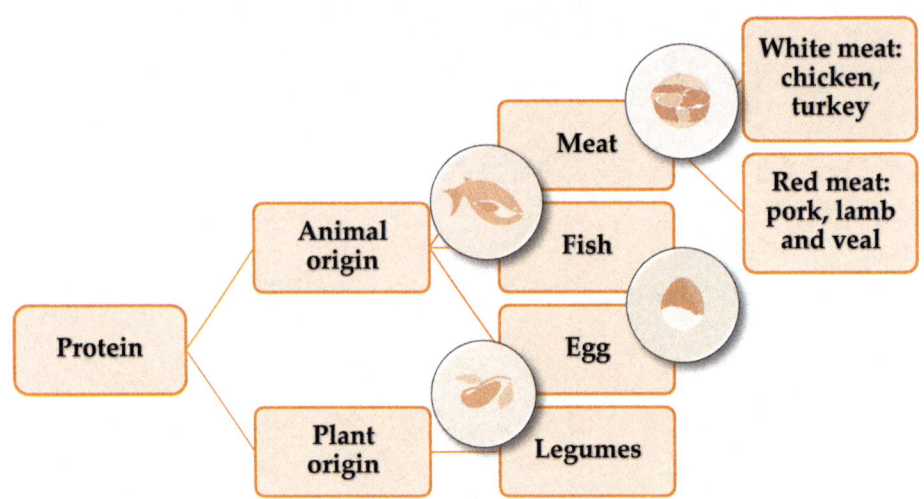

| Protein | Maximum Daily Quantity | Frequency of Consumption |
|---------|------------------------|--------------------------|
| Pork, lamb, veal | 30-35g | Only 1-2 times per week |
| Chicken, turkey | 30-35g | 2-3 times per week |
| Blue or white fish | 30-35g | 3-4 times per week |
| Egg | 1 egg size S/M | 3-4 times per week |
| Legumes | 60g cooked | Minimum 3-4 times per week |

This table will serve as a reference to ensure that you are offering your baby an adequate balance of nutrients throughout the week, without falling into monotony or excess of any particular food group. Remember that it is a flexible guideline and you can adjust it according to your preferences and those of your baby.

These are general guidelines and each baby has individual needs. Some may need more or fewer portions of certain food groups depending on their preferences, appetite, and growth rate. The important thing is to offer a wide variety of nutritious foods at each meal and allow your baby to decide how much to eat based on their cues of hunger and satiety.

### How many meals a day should I offer my baby?

During the first months of BLW, between 6 and 8 months, the ideal is to offer your baby opportunities to explore solid foods about 2-3 times a day. At this stage, breast milk or formula continues to be their main source of nutrition, and solids are more of a complement for your little one to discover new textures, flavors, and skills. From 9 months to 2 years, you can gradually increase the frequency of meals to about 3 - 4 times a day. Your baby will already be more accustomed to solids, and these will start gaining prominence in their diet, although milk will continue to be important until at least one year.

So, where to start with BLW? Here are some tips:

Initial stage of complementary feeding

6 - 8 months: offer easy-to-grasp preparations, such as:

o   Soft strips of meat: chicken, turkey, veal or lamb, well cooked and cut into strips that your baby can easily grasp.

o  Cooked vegetable sticks: broccoli, carrot, zucchini or sweet potatoes steamed or baked until soft.

o  Soft fruit pieces: ripe banana, avocado, ripe pear or mango, cut into easy-to-grasp chunks or wedges.

o  Well-cooked egg: hard-boiled eggs cut into quarters, or strips of omelet.

When preparing these first foods, keep in mind:

- Cook them until you can easily mash them with a fork, without them falling apart. This way they will have the ideal texture for your baby's gums.

- Cut the pieces to the appropriate size, roughly the size of their fist, so that your little one can safely and comfortably bring them to their mouth.

- Avoid adding salt, sugar or other condiments. Foods in their natural state already have the perfect flavor for a palate that is discovering the world. The less processed, the better!

### Later stage of complementary feeding initiation

8 - 9 months: once your baby has tried several foods separately and is getting better at handling them, you can start offering simple recipes combining a few ingredients. For example, zucchini omelet, chicken and carrot meatballs, or a thick lentil and couscous puree.

Stage from 9 - 12 months in feeding: At this stage your baby has much better mastery of the pincer grasp and is able to chew and swallow more varied textures. It is time to offer them more elaborate recipes with more ingredients, always adapted to their development and in a relaxed and positive environment.

For example, you can prepare vegetable lasagna, homemade legume burgers, quinoa pancakes with fruit, or a creamy risotto with fish chunks. Use your creativity to present them with appetizing, colorful and nutritious dishes, but without pressuring them or stressing yourself out. Remember, BLW is a mutual learning process in which enjoyment and respect for your baby's rhythm take precedence!

So now you know: start by offering your little one those first foods in soft, easy-to-grab pieces, and gradually introduce more complete and varied recipes.

## Plate method

This is a visual and practical way to make sure you offer your BLW baby an adequate variety of nutrients at each meal. It consists of imagining a plate divided into three parts:

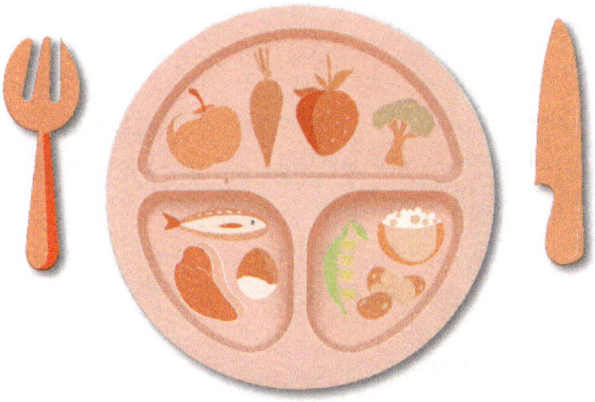

- o 1/2 of the plate: Fruits and vegetables. This is where all that wide range of colors and textures we mentioned before comes in. You can offer anything from strips of avocado or orange wedges to steamed broccoli or sweet potato slices.
- o 1/4 of the plate: Proteins. This is the place for those portions of shredded chicken, those lentil meatballs or those bits of omelet.
- o 1/4 of the plate: Carbohydrates. This is where those sticks of whole-grain bread, that pasta in the shape of letters, or those wedges of cooked potato come in.

This method is just a rough guide, not a strict rule. Each baby is unique and yours may need more or less of certain food groups depending on their appetite, growth rate, and preferences. In addition, it is not essential that each individual meal respect these proportions, but rather to seek a balance throughout the day and week.

The really important thing is to offer healthy and varied options at each opportunity and trust your baby's innate ability to self-regulate and eat according to their needs. The plate is a blank canvas that you can fill with the colors, flavors and textures that most appeal to and inspire you at each moment. Let your culinary creativity fly and enjoy this process of discovery together with your little one!

# Key points

o *Offer nutrient-rich, soft and easy-to-grasp foods, especially those high in iron and zinc.*

o *Ensure adequate iron intake through foods of animal and plant origin, combined with vitamin C sources.*

o *Include a wide variety of seasonal fruits and vegetables to expose the baby to different flavors, textures and nutrients.*

o *Provide 1-2 daily portions of protein foods, adapting the quantities to the baby's individual needs.*

o *Start with 2-3 opportunities for solid feeding per day between 6-8 months, and gradually increase to 3-4 times per day from 9-12 months, always respecting the baby's cues.*

# Chapter 5: Size, Shape and Texture: The Key to BLW Success

*"Details are not details. They make the design." - Charles Eames.*

The famous French gastronome Brillat-Savarin used to say: "Tell me how you cut and I will tell you who you are". And if this maxim applies to adult gourmets, imagine how much more so to babies starting out in the fascinating world of solid food! In BLW, the size, shape and texture of foods are much more than an aesthetic issue or a matter of protocol: they are the key to ensuring a safe, enjoyable and nutritious experience at each stage of development.

One of the most important aspects of BLW is making sure that the foods you offer your baby are of a size, shape and texture appropriate to their age and abilities. This will not only make the BLW experience safer and more enjoyable for your little one, but will also allow them to develop chewing, manipulation and self-feeding skills, naturally and progressively.

## Guide to Appropriate Sizes and Shapes for Each Stage

As your baby grows and develops new skills, the way you prepare and present foods will evolve. Here we offer a general guide to the recommended sizes and shapes for each stage of BLW:

### From 6 to 7 months:

o Sticks or strips the size of your baby's fist (roughly the size and thickness of your index finger).

- Soft foods that can be easily mashed with the gums.

- Avoid hard, small or round foods that may pose a choking hazard.

Examples: Steamed zucchini sticks, avocado wedges, ripe pear strips.

## From 7 to 9 months:

- Smaller pieces, the size of an almond or a small grape.

- Slightly firmer foods that require some chewing.

- Introduce foods with more varied textures, such as cooked rice or pasta.

Examples: Baked sweet potato cubes, banana slices, cooked chicken chunks.

## From 9 to 12 months:

Even smaller pieces, the size of a pea or a raisin.

More challenging foods that require more advanced chewing.

Offer a wide variety of textures, from lumpy purees to soft foods in small pieces.

Examples: Cooked peas, ground meat, bow tie pasta, fruit in small cubes.

| 6 - 8 Months | 9 Months |
| --- | --- |

## Progressing from Soft to Firmer and More Challenging

It is important to remember that each baby develops at their own pace, so this guide that I have prepared with an incalculable enthusiasm should be used as a reference and not as a strict rule.

At the beginning, it is essential to offer soft foods that your baby can easily mash with their gums, such as well-cooked fruits and vegetables, tender meats and flaked fish. As your little one gains more practice and confidence, you can gradually introduce slightly firmer foods with more varied textures.

An easy and quick way to check is by doing the "thumb test": press the food with the pad of your thumb and see if it mashes easily without much effort. If it mashes easily, it is likely to be safe and manageable for your baby. If it is too hard or firm, you can cook it a little more or cut it into smaller pieces.

It is important to note that the shapes and sizes are only rough guidelines, and that the fundamental thing is that both you and your baby feel comfortable and safe with the foods you offer. If a certain shape or texture doesn't work, don't hesitate to try something different. BLW is a mutual learning process, and it is normal for there to be some trial and error until you find what works best for your little one.

Also keep in mind that your baby's teething should not condition the foods you offer. Although it may seem surprising, babies' gums are strong enough to handle a wide variety of textures, even before the first teeth appear. In fact, the process of chewing and manipulating food with the gums is beneficial for the development of the jaw and oral muscles.

Of course, as teeth come in, you can start offering your baby slightly firmer and more challenging foods. But there is no need to wait until they have a full set of teeth to introduce certain textures. The key is to progress gradually and always under supervision, making sure your baby can handle the foods safely and comfortably.

# DID YOU KNOW THAT THE TEETHING PROCESS IS LIKE A JOURNEY FULL OF MILESTONES AND DISCOVERIES?
## LET'S EXPLORE THEM TOGETHER!

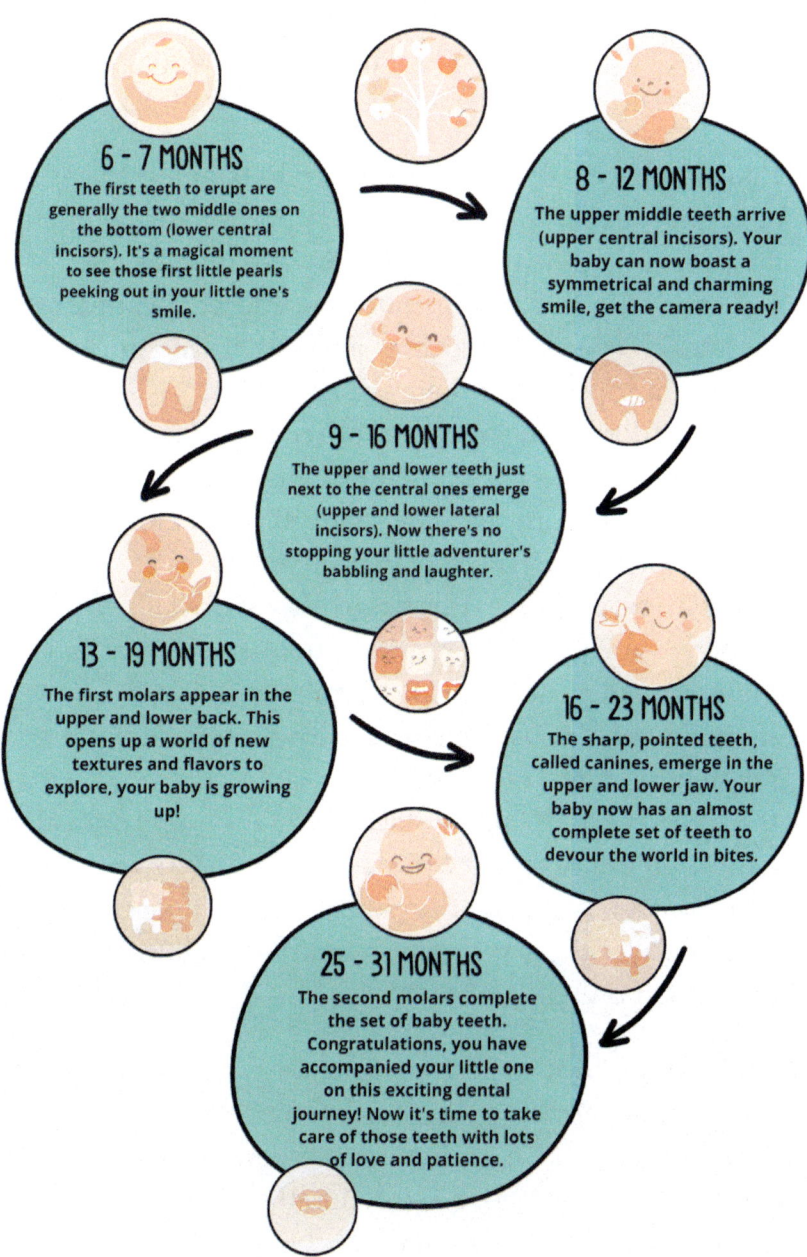

**6 - 7 MONTHS**
The first teeth to erupt are generally the two middle ones on the bottom (lower central incisors). It's a magical moment to see those first little pearls peeking out in your little one's smile.

**8 - 12 MONTHS**
The upper middle teeth arrive (upper central incisors). Your baby can now boast a symmetrical and charming smile, get the camera ready!

**9 - 16 MONTHS**
The upper and lower teeth just next to the central ones emerge (upper and lower lateral incisors). Now there's no stopping your little adventurer's babbling and laughter.

**13 - 19 MONTHS**
The first molars appear in the upper and lower back. This opens up a world of new textures and flavors to explore, your baby is growing up!

**16 - 23 MONTHS**
The sharp, pointed teeth, called canines, emerge in the upper and lower jaw. Your baby now has an almost complete set of teeth to devour the world in bites.

**25 - 31 MONTHS**
The second molars complete the set of baby teeth. Congratulations, you have accompanied your little one on this exciting dental journey! Now it's time to take care of those teeth with lots of love and patience.

## Tips for Adapting Family Foods to BLW

One of the great benefits of BLW is that it allows your baby to participate in family meals and explore the same foods that the rest of the family consumes. However, you may need to make some adaptations to ensure that these foods are safe and appropriate for your little one. Here are some tips:

1. **Cook foods until soft:** If your family is going to eat steamed or grilled vegetables, cook an extra portion for your baby until it is soft enough for them to mash with their gums.
2. **Cut food into the appropriate size and shape:** Before serving the meal, separate a portion and cut it into sticks, strips or pieces appropriate for their age and skills.
3. **Avoid adding salt, sugar and other condiments:** Food should be as natural as possible, without added salt, sugar or seasoning. You can separate their portion before adding these ingredients to the rest of the family meal.
4. **Offer a variety of textures and flavors:** As they progress in BLW, you can start offering them small portions of the different components of the family meal, such as rice, pasta, stews or casseroles. This will allow them to explore a wide range of textures and flavors.
5. **Get creative with presentations:** If the family meal doesn't lend itself easily to BLW (for example, a soup or a dish with a lot of sauce), you can offer your baby some of the ingredients separately, such as pieces of cooked vegetables, strips of meat or slices of bread.

Another important aspect to consider is how to safely store prepared foods for your BLW baby. Since it is common to cook extra portions to have on hand in case of need, it is essential to know how long they can be stored in the refrigerator and freezer without losing quality or safety.

| Food | Refrigerator storage | Freezer storage |
|---|---|---|
| Cooked fruits and vegetables | 3-5 days | 6-8 months |
| Cooked meat, chicken or fish | 3-4 days | 2-6 months |
| Hard-boiled eggs | Up to 1 week | Not recommended |
| Cooked legumes | 3-5 days | 6-8 months |
| Homemade purees and porridges | 24-48 hours | 1-3 months |

Always remember to label the containers with the date of preparation and consume the oldest foods first. If you have any doubts about the freshness or safety of any preparation, it is better to discard it. Better safe than sorry, especially when it comes to your baby's delicate tummy.

By adapting foods to the appropriate size, shape and texture for each stage of development, and storing them safely, you will be setting the stage for a successful and enjoyable experience. With a little planning and creativity, you will see that it is possible to offer them a varied, nutritious and exciting diet, without the need to always cook separately or over-complicate your life.

# Key points

o *The size, shape and texture of foods are key to a safe, enjoyable and nutritious BLW experience. Adapt the presentation of foods according to your baby's age and abilities.*

o *Start with large, soft pieces (6-7 months), progress to smaller, firmer pieces (7-9 months), and finally offer more challenging and varied pieces (9-12 months). Use the "thumb test" to check for the right texture.*

o *The baby's teething should not condition the foods offered. Gums are strong enough to handle different textures even before teeth appear.*

o *To adapt family foods to BLW, cook them until soft, cut them to the appropriate size and shape, avoid adding salt, sugar and condiments, offer variety and be creative with presentations.*

o *Store prepared foods safely, labeling with the date and consuming the oldest ones first. When in doubt, it is better to discard.*

# Chapter 6: Food Allergies and Intolerances: Navigating Safely

*"Knowledge is power."* - *Francis Bacon*

If you've made it this far, you probably already know that Baby-Led Weaning is much more than a simple complementary feeding method. But what happens when that process intersects with a word that chills many parents' blood: allergy? How do you approach BLW when your baby has or may have an adverse reaction to certain foods? Is it possible to follow this approach when there are dietary restrictions or precautions to take? Or is it better to throw in the towel and go back to the "safe" purees and jars?

If these questions resonate with you or generate anxiety, I want you to take a deep breath and calm down. Because the answer is clear and forceful: of course it is possible to do BLW with an allergic or intolerant baby! In fact, not only is it possible, but it can even be beneficial in preventing or better managing these conditions, as long as it is done in an informed, individualized manner and under pediatric supervision.

In this chapter, we will explore in detail how to address the issue of allergies and intolerances in the context of BLW, from prevention to management, including diagnosis and adaptation. But before diving into the topic, allow me to remind you of some key concepts that are sometimes confused or used interchangeably:

o A food allergy is an adverse reaction of the immune system to a protein present in a food, which the body mistakenly identifies as a threat. Symptoms can be cutaneous (hives, swelling, itching), digestive (vomiting, diarrhea, abdominal pain), respiratory (cough, difficulty breathing) or systemic (anaphylaxis). The most common allergies in infants and children are to egg, milk, wheat, soy, fish, shellfish, nuts and peanuts.

o A food intolerance is an adverse reaction to a food that does not involve the immune system, but is due to the body's inability to properly digest or metabolize certain components. Symptoms are usually mainly digestive (gas, bloating, abdominal pain, diarrhea) and do not pose a life-threatening risk. The most common intolerances are to lactose (the sugar in milk) and gluten (a protein present in wheat, barley, rye and oats).

o Celiac disease is an autoimmune disease triggered by the consumption of gluten in genetically predisposed people. It is not an allergy or an intolerance per se, but a chronic condition that mainly affects the small intestine and requires a strict gluten-free diet for life.

It is important to distinguish these conditions because their approach and prognosis are different. While some allergies (such as egg or milk) tend to be transient and are outgrown over time, others (such as peanuts or shellfish) tend to be persistent and require lifelong avoidance. Intolerances, on the other hand, can vary in their intensity and duration, and sometimes the problematic foods can be reintroduced gradually and in a controlled manner. And celiac disease, as we have said, implies a permanent gluten-free diet to avoid damage to health.

In any case, if you suspect that your baby may have an allergy, an intolerance or celiac disease, it is essential that you consult with your pediatrician or a pediatric allergy specialist. They will be able to perform the necessary diagnostic tests (such as blood tests, skin tests or oral provocations) and offer you the specific treatment and follow-up guidelines for your particular case.

Once these concepts are clarified, let's see how we can adapt BLW to each situation, starting with prevention. Because yes, prevention of food allergies starts in BLW!

## Introduction of Major Allergens: Latest Recommendations

In the past, it was recommended to delay the introduction of potentially allergenic foods, such as egg, fish, gluten and nuts, until after the first year of life. However, more recent research has shown that delaying the introduction of these foods does not prevent allergies and, in fact, could even increase the risk of developing them.

Currently, the American Academy of Pediatrics (AAP), along with the National Institute of Allergy and Infectious Diseases (NIAID) and other leading medical organizations, recommend introducing potentially allergenic foods between 4 and 6 months of age, similar to the introduction of other solid foods. This recommendation applies to all infants, including those at higher risk of allergies due to factors such as family history. The main food allergens include:

| Fish | Shellfish | Egg |
|------|-----------|-----|
| Gluten | Soy | Sesame |
| Peanuts | Tree nuts | Dairy |

When introducing these foods, it is important to do so one at a time, in small amounts and being attentive to any signs of allergic reaction. If your baby tolerates the food without problems, you can gradually increase the quantity and give it to them more often.

The "3-day rule" is an excellent guideline to follow when introducing a new potentially allergenic food. Offer the food for three consecutive days, closely observing for any reaction. If there are no symptoms, you can assume that your baby is not allergic to that particular food and continue to include it in their diet on a regular basis.

If you suspect a possible allergy, it is crucial to remove the food from the diet and consult with your pediatrician before reintroducing it. Remember that the allergic reaction may not be immediate, so it is important to be attentive to symptoms up to 48 hours after ingestion. Another important recommendation is not to introduce potentially allergenic foods at night, as it may be more difficult to detect and respond to a reaction while your baby is sleeping. It is better to offer them during the day, when you can closely observe your little one and act quickly if necessary.

Regarding the benefits of breast milk in the prevention of allergies, some studies *(American Academy of Pediatrics (2012) Breastfeeding and the use of human milk. Pediatrics, 129(3), e827-e841)* conclude that exclusive breastfeeding during the first 4-6 months of life may have a protective effect, especially in high-risk children. This is because breast milk contains a wide variety of immunological components, such as antibodies, cytokines and prebiotics, which modulate the baby's immune response and promote the development of a healthy intestinal microbiota.

In addition, it has been seen that early exposure to small amounts of allergens through breast milk may promote oral tolerance in the baby. Therefore, unless there is a confirmed allergy in the mother or baby, it is not necessary for the breastfeeding woman to avoid potentially allergenic foods during lactation.

Of course, if your baby has already been diagnosed with a food allergy or intolerance, the story is different. In that case, it is essential that you work closely with your pediatrician or allergist to identify the foods your baby should avoid and make sure their diet remains complete and nutritious. But don't worry, BLW remains an appropriate and beneficial option for most babies with allergies, as long as the necessary precautions are taken.

## Identifying and Responding to Allergic Reactions

Despite the fact that food allergies are relatively rare (affecting 5-8% of children), it is crucial to know how to recognize the symptoms of an allergic reaction and how to act in case it occurs. Symptoms can appear from minutes to several hours after ingestion of the food and may include:

| | | |
|---|---|---|
| Urticaria, rash, or swelling of the face, tongue, or lips | Nausea, vomiting, or diarrhea | Difficulty breathing, wheezing, or persistent cough |
| Itching or redness of the skin, eyes, or mouth | Abdominal pain or cramps | Dizziness or loss of consciousness (in severe cases of anaphylaxis) |

If you suspect that your baby is having an allergic reaction:

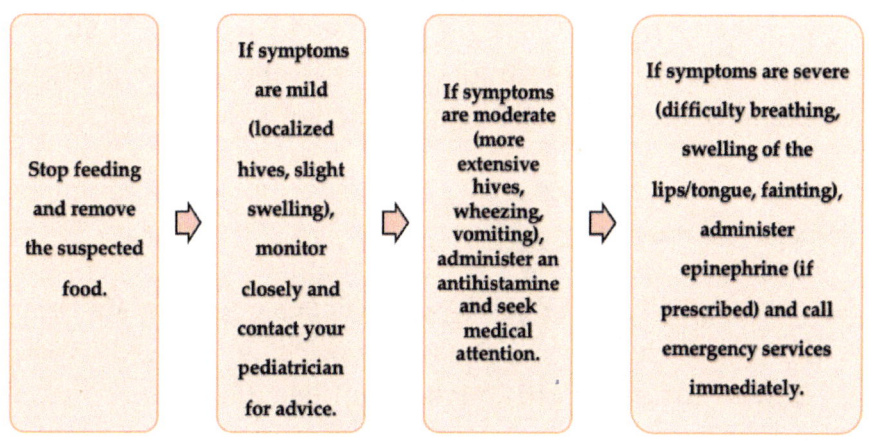

After an allergic reaction, it is important to follow the instructions of your pediatrician or allergist on how to reintroduce or avoid the food in question. Additional tests may be necessary to confirm the allergy and develop a long-term management plan.

In the case of food intolerances, symptoms tend to be less severe and more related to the digestive system, such as abdominal pain, gas, diarrhea or constipation. The most common intolerances in infants and young children are lactose intolerance (to the sugar in milk) and gluten intolerance (a protein present in wheat, barley and rye). Unlike allergies, intolerances do not involve a reaction of the immune system, but rather a difficulty in digesting or absorbing certain components of foods. In many cases, symptoms of intolerance improve or disappear when the problematic food is removed from the diet and reintroduced gradually in a controlled manner. If you suspect that your baby may have an intolerance, it is best to consult with your pediatrician for diagnosis and specific treatment guidelines.

## BLW for Babies with Known Allergies or Intolerances

If your baby has been diagnosed with a food allergy or intolerance, you may wonder if Baby-Led Weaning is a safe and appropriate option. The good news is that, with some adaptations and precautions, most babies with allergies or intolerances can perfectly enjoy its benefits.

Here are some tips to make BLW a safe and enjoyable experience for your baby:

1. **Work closely with your pediatrician or allergist:** They can help you identify which foods your baby should avoid and how to ensure a nutritionally complete diet.

2. **Read food labels carefully:** Make sure the products you offer your baby do not contain the allergen in question, including traces of cross-contamination.

3. **Prepare separate meals:** If the rest of the family consumes foods that your baby should avoid, prepare separate meals for your little one to avoid the risk of cross-contamination. It is important to maintain good hand hygiene and hygiene of utensils and kitchen surfaces where food is prepared.

4. **Offer safe and nutritious alternatives:** Look for foods that can nutritionally replace those your baby cannot consume. For example, if your baby is allergic to cow's milk, you can offer extensively hydrolyzed or amino acid-based formulas, as well as calcium from other sources such as green leafy vegetables or fortified products.

In the specific case of egg allergy, the following image shows how to substitute it:

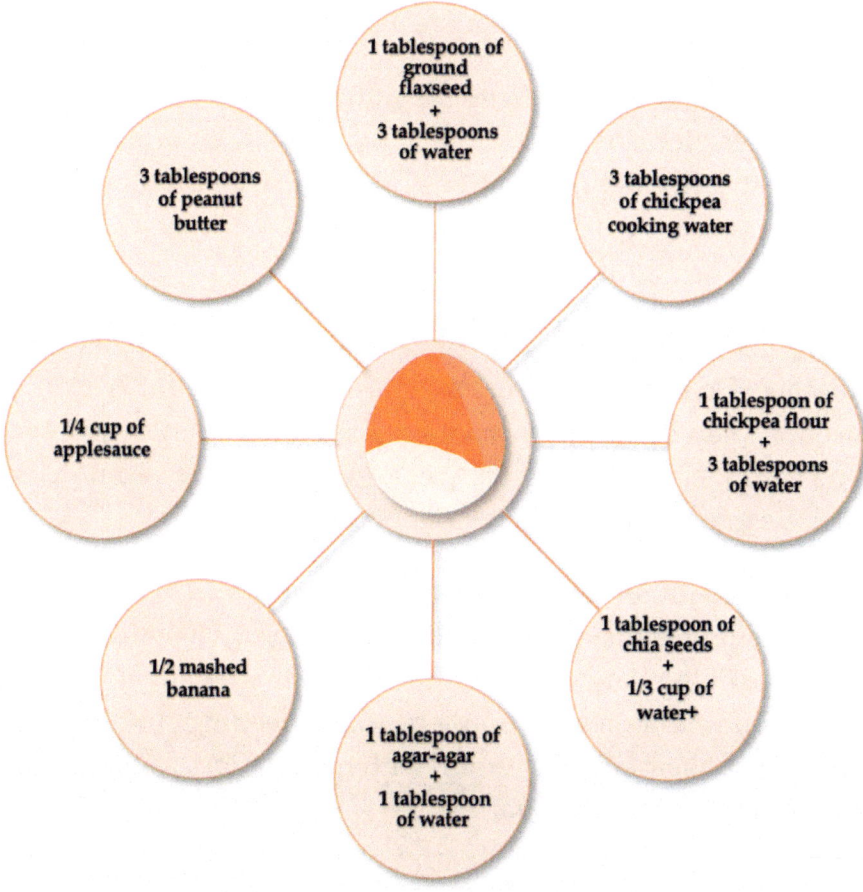

Other safe and nutritious alternatives for babies with allergies or intolerances are products specially formulated for them, such as cookies, cereals or porridges that are free of the most common allergens. However, keep in mind that these products can be quite expensive and that, in general, it is preferable to opt for natural and minimally processed foods whenever possible.

o **Educate other caregivers:** If your baby is in the care of other people (grandparents, caregivers, educators), make sure they are informed about their allergies or intolerances and know how to prevent and recognize a reaction

o **Keep a food record:** Write down the foods you introduce and any reactions you observe. This can help you and your pediatrician identify patterns and adjust your baby's feeding plan as needed.

In short, each baby is different and the severity and type of allergic or intolerance reactions can vary greatly from one case to another. Don't be afraid to ask questions or ask for help if you need it. With information, caution and a little culinary creativity, you can ensure that your baby enjoys a safe, tasty and nutritious diet, despite their dietary restrictions.

Another important aspect to consider when we talk about allergies and intolerances in BLW are digestive symptoms and their possible relationship with feeding. It is relatively common for babies who start complementary feeding to experience changes in their bowel rhythm, with more or less frequent, softer or harder stools than usual.

In most cases, these changes are a normal part of the process of adaptation to new foods and should not be a cause for concern. However, if you notice that your baby has symptoms such as persistent diarrhea, severe constipation, blood in stools, recurrent vomiting or lack of weight gain, it is important that you consult with your pediatrician to rule out possible medical causes, including allergies or intolerances. Your pediatrician may request specific tests to confirm or rule out an allergy or intolerance.

Your little one is much more than their dietary restrictions. With your love, patience and dedication, they will be able to develop a healthy and positive relationship with food, despite the challenges they may encounter along the way. And who knows? Perhaps this experience will inspire you to also explore new ingredients, flavors and recipes that you would never have tried otherwise.

# Key points

o *According to the latest recommendations, potentially allergenic foods should be introduced between 4 and 6 months, just like other solid foods, to promote immunological tolerance.*

o *When introducing potentially allergenic foods, it is important to do so one at a time, in small amounts, and monitor for any reaction for about 48 hours. The "3-day rule" is a good guideline to follow.*

o *If you suspect an allergic reaction in your baby, stop feeding, remove the suspected food and seek medical attention if symptoms are severe or do not improve. In case of anaphylaxis, administer adrenaline and call emergency services.*

o *Babies with known allergies or intolerances can still benefit from BLW, as long as precautions are taken such as strictly avoiding problematic foods, offering safe and nutritious alternatives, and educating all caregivers.*

o *Digestive symptoms are common during the introduction of solids, but some may indicate a possible allergy or intolerance. Keep your pediatrician updated and consult any doubts.*

# PART III:

# OVERCOMING COMMON BLW CHALLENGES

# Chapter 7: Addressing the Fear of Choking

*"Fear is an underestimated teacher." - Jim Morrison*

In this chapter I want to invite you to explore some of the most common fears and challenges that usually arise in BLW, and to find tools and perspectives to overcome them. One of the most common fears among parents considering Baby-Led Weaning is the possibility of their baby choking on pieces of solid food.

## Understanding the Difference between Gagging and Choking

| Gagging | Choking |
|---|---|
| • When a piece of food touches the back of the tongue or throat before the baby is ready to swallow it, the gag reflex pushes the tongue forward to expel the food.. | • Occurs when an object completely or partially blocks the airway, making it difficult or impossible to breathe. |
| • During gagging, the baby may make noises, turn red, and have expression of discomfort. | • The baby cannot cough, cry, or make any noise. |
| • During gagging, the baby continues to breathe and can resolve it on their own. | • The skin may start to turn blue around the lips and nails. |
| • No intervention is required. | • It is a medical emergency that requires immediate intervention. |
| • It is a natural protective reflex to prevent choking. | |

Gagging and choking are two distinct phenomena, and it is crucial to know how to distinguish them in order to respond appropriately in each situation:

- **Gagging:** Gagging is a natural protective reflex that helps prevent choking. When a piece of food touches the back of the tongue or throat before the baby is ready to swallow it, the gag reflex pushes the tongue forward to expel the food. During gagging, the baby may make noises, turn red, and have an expression of discomfort, but they continue to breathe and are able to resolve it on their own. It does not require intervention.

- **Choking:** Choking occurs when an object totally or partially blocks the airways, making breathing difficult or impossible. A baby who is choking will not be able to cough, cry or make noises, and their skin may start to turn blue around the lips and nails. This is a medical emergency that requires immediate intervention.

How to recognize gagging and choking, some signs are:

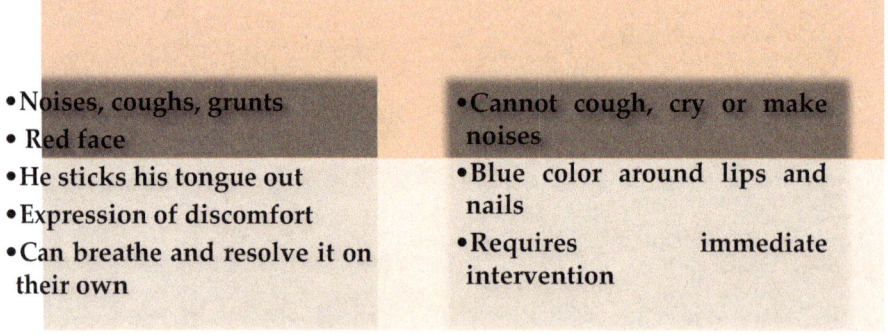

| |
|---|
| • Noises, coughs, grunts |
| • Red face |
| • He sticks his tongue out |
| • Expression of discomfort |
| • Can breathe and resolve it on their own |

| |
|---|
| • Cannot cough, cry or make noises |
| • Blue color around lips and nails |
| • Requires immediate intervention |

Always keep in mind that gagging is a normal, protective reflex. Although it can be alarming to see, try to stay calm and allow your baby to resolve the gag on their own.

Intervening unnecessarily can be counterproductive and increase the risk of actual choking. Unlike gagging, with signs of true choking it is crucial to act immediately, both with first aid techniques and by calling emergency services: in USA the emergency number is 911, in Australia 112, and in UK 999.

## Key First Aid Techniques for Safe Feeding

Although choking situations are rare when following BLW safety guidelines, it is essential that all caregivers know how to act in an emergency. Here we present some key first aid techniques:

### Heimlich Maneuver

The Heimlich maneuver is a first aid technique used to clear the airways of a person who is choking. Here we explain how to perform it on babies:

1. Place the baby face down over your forearm, with the head lower than the chest. Support their jaw with your hand and rest your forearm on your thigh.

2. With the base of the other hand, give up to 5 firm and quick blows in the middle of the baby's back, between the shoulder blades.

3. If the back blows do not clear the obstruction, turn the baby face up onto your other forearm, with the head lower than the chest. Using two fingers, perform up to 5 chest compressions in the center of the chest, just below the nipple line. The compressions should be quick and approximately 1.5 inches deep.

4. If the obstruction is still not cleared, continue alternating 5 back blows with 5 chest compressions until the object is expelled or the baby loses consciousness.

5. If the baby loses consciousness, call emergency services immediately and begin pediatric CPR if you are trained to do so.

It is highly recommended that all caregivers take a practical pediatric first aid course to learn and practice these lifesaving techniques. However, in an emergency, it is better to act following these guidelines than to do nothing at all. Remember that prevention is always the best strategy.

## Strategies for Managing Parental Anxiety

It is normal to feel some anxiety when starting with BLW, especially around the risk of choking. However, there are several strategies you can use to manage these fears and enjoy the process more:

1. **Educate yourself**: Learn, research and read everything you can about BLW, including safety guidelines, appropriate food sizes and textures, and first aid techniques. The more informed you are, the more confident you will feel.

2. **Start slow**: You don't have to jump into BLW headfirst from day one. You can start by offering a single soft food at each meal and gradually add more variety and textures as you and your baby feel more comfortable. Remember that you should always feel at ease with the process. If something generates a lot of anxiety for you, give it time and go slowly. This was the key point for me: there was a before and after since I approached it with this vision.

3. **Trust your baby**: They have strong survival instincts and protective reflexes. Observe how they handle the pieces, how they chew and swallow, and how they self-regulate. You will see that they are much more capable than you imagine.

4. **Create a calm environment**: Try to keep meals relaxed and free of distractions. Avoid eating in a hurry or with anxiety, as your baby may perceive and absorb those emotions.

5. **Connect with other parents**: Join family groups where you can share your experiences and concerns with others who practice BLW.

6. **Seek professional support**: If your anxiety around BLW interferes with your ability to enjoy meals, consider psychologists and therapists specializing in maternity and parenting, who can help you develop personalized strategies to manage your fears and foster a healthy bond with your baby during meals.

The fear of choking is a common and understandable fear among parents, but it should not stop you from exploring the many benefits of Baby-Led Weaning. With information, preparation and a positive attitude, you will be able to gradually let go of that anxiety and enjoy more and more this exciting stage in your baby's development.

## Foods that Require Special Attention

Although most foods can be safely adapted for BLW, there are some that deserve special considerations due to their shape, size or consistency:

| Food | How to offer | How to avoid |
| --- | --- | --- |
| Grapes, cherry tomatoes, large berries | Cut longitudinally and then into quarters before offering | Never give whole, as their round shape and firm skin make them especially prone to getting stuck in the throat. |
| Sausages, hot dogs and other cold cuts | Cut lengthwise and then into small pieces | Avoid offering in coin or circle shape, as they can easily block the airways. |
| Carrot sticks, celery and other hard vegetables | Cook until very soft and cut into small pieces | Avoid offering raw and in long sticks, as they can break into hard, sharp pieces that can damage gums or get stuck in the throat. |
| Peanut butter and other nut butters | Offer spread in thin layers on toast or crackers | Avoid giving large spoonfuls that can stick to the palate and be difficult for your baby to handle |
| Hard candies, gum and popcorn | | Avoid completely until your child is at least 4-5 years old and has perfected their chewing and swallowing skills. |
| Whole nuts and seeds | Grind or mill finely before offering, for example, sprinkled on yogurt or mixed into cookie dough | Avoid giving whole until your child is older and can chew them effectively. In addition to being a choking hazard, they are also one of the most common allergens. |
| Raw apples and pears | Grate or cook until soft | Avoid offering hard pieces that can break into small, sharp pieces that the baby can choke on. |
| Foods with sticks or bones | Always make sure to remove sticks, wires and bones before giving the pieces of food to your baby. | Avoid offering skewers, Moorish skewers, chicken drumsticks with bones, lamb chops, etc. Fish bones are especially dangerous due to their small size and sharp points. |

In general, always use your best judgment and common sense when preparing and offering foods to your BLW baby. If you have any doubts about a particular product, consult your pediatrician or an expert in infant nutrition. So take this chapter not as a list of prohibitions, but as an invitation to be mindful, to use common sense, and to trust the process.

## Key points

o *Neophobia or initial rejection of new foods is a normal and adaptive response in babies, which is overcome with patience, repeated exposure and a positive environment around food.*

o *Gagging and choking are two different phenomena. Gagging is a normal protective reflex, while choking is an emergency that requires immediate intervention.*

o *Learn to recognize the signs of gagging (noises, redness, expression of discomfort, but with breathing) and choking (inability to cough, cry or breathe, bluish color on lips and nails).*

o *Familiarize yourself with first aid techniques, such as the Heimlich maneuver, to act quickly in case of choking. It is recommended to take a practical course.*

o *To manage anxiety around BLW, mentally anticipate, respond with humor and assertiveness, offer brief and positive information, set boundaries if necessary, and focus on enjoying the moment with your family.*

o *Some foods require special preparation to avoid risks, such as cutting grapes and sausages longitudinally and into small pieces, cooking hard vegetables well, spreading nuts thinly, and avoiding hard and sticky foods until 4-5 years of age*

# Chapter 8: When Your Baby Seems to Not Want Certain Foods

*"Patience is bitter, but its fruit is sweet." - Jean-Jacques Rousseau*

As your little one explores the world of solid foods through BLW, it is likely that they will encounter some flavors or textures that they don't like right away. This is completely normal and doesn't mean that your baby is a "bad eater". In fact, initial rejection of certain foods is an evolutionary protective mechanism that deters babies from ingesting potentially dangerous substances.

However, with patience, persistence, and a relaxed approach, most babies end up expanding their preferences and accepting a wide variety of foods.

## The Power of Repeated Exposure and Patience

Studies *(Forestell, C. A. (2017).)* have shown that babies may need up to 15-20 exposures to a new food before fully accepting it. This is because food neophobia, or fear of new foods, is an inherited trait that protects babies from ingesting potentially toxic or harmful foods.

It is a normal and healthy response that dates back to our hunter-gatherer ancestors, for whom trying an unknown food could be a matter of life or death. But in the current context, where most of the foods we offer our babies are safe and nutritious, this neophobia can be frustrating and discouraging for parents.

It is easy to interpret the baby's rejection as a personal failure or a sign that something is wrong. However, it is important to remember that this behavior is temporary and does not reflect parenting skills or define the child's future eating habits. With time and repeated exposure, what was once "new and scary" becomes "familiar and safe". The baby learns that this food is part of their usual food environment and does not represent a threat. And one day, almost without realizing it, they try it and discover that it's not so bad. They may even end up liking it.

This process can take days, weeks or even months, depending on the baby and the food in question. There are studies that suggest that babies take longer to accept bitter vegetables such as kale, while sweet foods such as fruits are usually easier to introduce. So, if your baby rejects a food the first, second or tenth time, don't get discouraged. Keep offering it on different occasions and preparations, without pressure or drama. Let them explore it with all their senses, even if they don't eat it. And, above all, don't force them or remove it definitively from the menu. Give them time and space to get used to that food at their own pace.

Some practical strategies to encourage acceptance of new foods through repeated exposure include:

1. Serve small amounts of the **new food along with others already known** and accepted. For example, if your baby loves steamed zucchini sticks, you can add a few slices of eggplant on the same plate. The familiarity of a favorite food can help "camouflage" the new food and make it more attractive.

2. Offer the same food in **different forms and textures**. For example, if your baby shows no interest in slices of raw tomato, try offering it pureed, in soup, roasted or in sauce. Sometimes, the same vegetable or fruit prepared in another way is much more appetizing.

3. **Involve your baby** in the preparation of meals whenever possible. For example, let them "help" you wash and mix the ingredients, knead the dough for some cookies, or distribute the food on their plate. The more they participate in the process, the more interest and curiosity they will show in trying the final result.

4. Make the **presentations** of the dishes more **attractive** and **fun**. Use shaped molds, create faces or landscapes with the food, decorate the plates with colorful edible elements.

5. **Be a good role model**, eating the same foods you offer your baby with evident pleasure and enthusiasm. Babies learn by imitation, so if they see you enjoying a wide variety of healthy foods, they are more likely to want to try them too. Take advantage of family meals to show them that eating is a social, enjoyable and nutritious act.

6. **Avoid** the temptation to always prepare **the same** "safe" **foods** that you know they like. It is normal to want to avoid rejection and food waste, but in the long run this can limit the variety in the baby's diet and reinforce neophobia. Keep offering their favorite dishes, but try to regularly introduce new or less accepted foods.

And if, despite your efforts and patience, you notice that your baby continues to have a very limited repertoire of foods or reacts with much anxiety or rejection to meals, do not hesitate to consult with your pediatrician. In some cases, there may be sensory, digestive or developmental factors that require a more specialized approach.

## Tricks to Encourage Acceptance of New Flavors and Textures

In addition to repeated exposure in a relaxed context, there are several tricks and strategies that you can use to make new or less preferred foods more attractive and easier for your baby to accept. Here are some of the most effective:

1. Combine the new with the known and the sweet with the bitter. For example, if your baby has trouble accepting bitter vegetables like arugula, try mixing them with others they like more, such as sweet potato or carrot. Or prepare a combined puree of fruits and vegetables, such as apple and broccoli or pear and zucchini. The contrast of flavors can make less appetizing foods more interesting.

2. Play with temperatures and sensations in the mouth. Some babies are very attracted to cold foods, such as fruit purees frozen in molds, vegetable sorbets or chilled cucumber slices. Others love crunchy textures, such as toasted bread sticks or crunchy chickpeas in the oven. Experiment with different temperatures and consistencies to see which ones arouse your baby's curiosity the most.

3. Use mild condiments and spices to enhance the flavor of foods. Although we should avoid added salt and sugar, we can use other natural and healthy flavor enhancers, such as fresh herbs (parsley, basil, mint), mild spices (cinnamon, nutmeg, cumin), citrus (lemon or orange juice), or dressings like extra virgin olive oil or tahini. A touch of these ingredients can transform a bland dish into an explosion of flavor.

4. Offer new or less preferred foods at the beginning of the meal, when your baby is hungrier and more receptive. If you wait until the end, when they are already full or tired, they are more likely to reject them after barely trying them. Take advantage of those first minutes of "curious appetite" to introduce the most challenging foods.

5. Present less popular foods in fun and visually appealing formats. For example, cut vegetables into geometric shapes with cookie cutters, mount colorful fruit skewers, or use molds to make fish burgers or homemade chicken "nuggets". The more appetizing the food looks, the more your baby will want to explore it.

6. Involve other children or adults that your baby admires in tasting new foods. Sometimes, seeing an older sibling, cousin or little friend enjoy a meal with enthusiasm can be the best incentive for your baby to try it too. Take advantage of social and family occasions to expose them to different models of healthy eating.

That said, it is important to remember that, no matter how creative and attractive our strategies are, we cannot and should not force a baby to eat something they don't want. If, after several attempts and exposures, your little one continues to consistently reject a food, respect it. They may simply not like that particular flavor or texture, or they may not yet be mature enough to appreciate it. And that's okay.

It's not about your baby becoming an early "foodie" or liking absolutely all foods. It's about developing a positive and healthy relationship with food, based on curiosity, respect for their internal sensations and enjoyment without prejudice. And that, like so many other things in parenting, is a gradual and unique process for each child.

Speaking of food preferences, I can't end this chapter without mentioning one of the biggest fears of parents who practice BLW: what if my baby only wants to eat carbohydrates? What if they systematically reject proteins or vegetables? Will they be getting all the nutrients they need?

Although it is normal to worry about the baby's nutritional intake, in general, if you follow the principles of BLW and offer a wide variety of healthy foods at each meal, you don't have to obsess over nutrient counting. Healthy, full-term babies have an innate ability to self-regulate their caloric intake and obtain the nutrients they need from a varied and complete diet.

It is true that some babies go through stages in which they clearly prefer certain food groups over others. For example, it is not uncommon for many children between 15-18 months to develop an intense predilection for carbohydrates and reject vegetables or proteins. This may be due to several factors, such as the soft texture and sweet taste of high-carbohydrate foods, increased neophobia at this age, or a slower growth rate that reduces the need for energy and nutrients.

But these phases are usually transitory and do not represent a nutritional problem in the long term, as long as we continue to offer all food groups at each meal, without restrictions or pressures. With time and repeated exposure in a positive environment, most children end up diversifying their diet and accepting a greater variety of foods.

Observe your baby, listen to their cues, respect their preferences. Because each new food tried, each texture experienced, each gesture of satisfaction or bewilderment, is one more step on their path towards autonomy and self-confidence. And that, my friends, is what is truly important. The rest are just details.

# Key points

- *Neophobia or initial rejection of new foods is a normal and adaptive response in babies, which is overcome with patience, repeated exposure and a positive environment around food.*

- *Some tricks to encourage acceptance of new foods are: combining the new with the known, playing with temperatures and textures, using spices and herbs, offering less preferred foods at the beginning of the meal, and presenting them in an attractive and fun way.*

- *Each baby has their own preferences and pace of food acceptance. Our role is to offer variety and a positive environment, but always respecting their individual cues and decisions.*

- *The true success of BLW is not that the baby eats everything, but that they develop a trusting and enjoyable relationship with food, respecting their instinct and autonomy.*

# Chapter 9: BLW Outside the Home: Yes, It's Possible!

*"Education is the most powerful weapon you can use to change the world." - Nelson Mandela*

One of the most attractive aspects of Baby-Led Weaning is that it allows your baby to fully participate in family and social meals, without the need to prepare special purees or foods. However, many parents are reluctant to apply BLW when eating away from home, whether in a restaurant, at friends' or relatives' homes, or while traveling.

They worry that the baby will not find suitable options on the menu, that they will get too dirty, that outsiders will judge them, or that it will be difficult to maintain the routine and principles of BLW in a different environment. And this is understandable: eating out with a baby is always a logistical and emotional challenge, regardless of the feeding method followed. But the good news is that, with a little planning, flexibility and sense of humor, it is totally possible and enjoyable in these situations.

## Tips for Eating in Restaurants or at Friends' Homes

Eating in a restaurant or at friends' homes with a baby who follows BLW may seem overwhelming at first, but with these tips, it can become a pleasant and relaxed experience for everyone:

1. **Choose the right place:** Look for family-friendly restaurants or cafes, with enough space for a high chair or stroller, and a relaxed and welcoming atmosphere. If you are going to friends' or relatives' homes, make sure they are comfortable with the BLW approach and with the inevitable mess that comes with it. Explain a little bit about what it consists of and why you have chosen it, so that it doesn't catch them by surprise.

2. **Make a strategic menu selection:** Before going to the restaurant, take a look at the menu online (if they have it) and look for dishes that are easy to adapt to BLW. Some options usually are: omelet, soft tacos or fajitas, pasta with light sauces, soupy rice, steamed or baked potatoes, grilled meats and fish, and of course, cooked fruits and vegetables as a side dish. Avoid fried foods, breaded items, very liquid sauces or very salty or spicy dishes.

3. **Ask for some simple adaptations:** When you place your order, don't hesitate to ask for small modifications that facilitate BLW. For example, not adding salt to the vegetables or potatoes, cooking the pasta or rice a little more so that it is softer, or serving the sauces on the side. Most restaurants are happy to customize dishes for little diners.

4. **Bring some foods and utensils from home:** To make sure your baby has something suitable to put in their mouth, it doesn't hurt to bring a small selection of BLW-friendly foods with you. Some ideas are: bread sticks or corn cakes, raw vegetable sticks (cucumber, carrot), fruit wedges (mango, avocado), cheese portions, chopped hard-boiled egg, or even some leftover homemade food. It is also useful to bring some utensils and tableware that your baby already knows and handles well, such as their favorite cup or mug, a silicone plate and spoon, a cloth napkin, etc.

5.  **Choose a good timing and a good location:** If possible, try to go to the restaurant at quiet times, when there are fewer people and noise. It is also preferable to sit in slightly secluded areas or with easy access to the outside, in case you need to go out to calm or change your baby. Make sure you bring everything you need in your bag (diapers, wipes, change of clothes, pacifier, small toys...) to be able to enjoy the meal with peace of mind. And if your baby is tired or sick that day, it may be better to postpone it and stay home.

6.  **Be realistic with your expectations:** Remember that eating out with a baby is always an adventure, so don't expect a perfect or controlled experience down to the millimeter. It is likely that your baby will eat less than usual (or more, if they are stimulated by the environment), that they will get quite dirty, that they will want to get up and explore, or that they will have a moment of crying or tantrum. All of that is normal and does not mean that BLW is not working or that your baby is behaving "badly". It is simply part of the learning and adaptation to new contexts. So, take a deep breath, smile and focus on enjoying the shared moment with your family.

### Portable and Easy-to-Prepare Meal Ideas

Another key aspect to succeed with BLW away from home is having a good repertoire of portable, easy-to-prepare meals that are suitable to take in a container or bag. That way, if you go for a picnic in the park, on a field trip or traveling by car or train, you will always have healthy and varied options on hand to offer your baby.

Some ideas for BLW meals to go are:

1. **Varied sandwiches and rolls:** avocado and cheese, hummus and roasted pepper, omelet and tomato, veggie pate and cucumber, peanut butter and banana... The combinations are endless. To make them more manageable, cut them into strips or quarters and wrap them.

2. **Wraps and rolls:** a base of corn or wheat tortilla, spread with cream cheese, pate or hummus and rolled with strips of vegetables and proteins, such as chicken, turkey, smoked salmon, scrambled egg, avocado, spinach... Wrap them tightly in plastic wrap and cut them into bite-sized portions.

3. **Fun skewers:** mount skewers with pieces of fruit (watermelon, melon, mango, banana), cheese cubes, mushrooms, cherry tomatoes, omelet cubes... Use pointless wooden sticks or silicone sticks for babies. You can also make mini skewers of grilled chicken or salmon, interspersed with steamed veggies.

4. **Vegetable frittatas and omelets:** beat a couple of eggs and add your favorite grated or chopped vegetables (zucchini, carrot, leek, pumpkin...), a little grated cheese and spices to taste. Pour the mixture into muffin molds or make small pancakes in the pan. When set, let them cool and store them in a container or airtight bag.

5. **Mini meatballs and burgers:** prepare your favorite homemade meatballs or burgers (meat, fish, legumes, vegetables...), but make them walnut-sized. This way they will be easy to pick up and eat in a couple of bites. You can serve them cold or heat them up a bit before leaving the house and put them in a thermos.

6. **Savory pancakes and waffles:** prepare a light batter with whole-wheat flour, egg, milk and a pinch of salt, and add savory ingredients such as grated cheese, bits of ham, herbs, chopped veggies... Make small waffles or pancakes and let them cool on a rack. They are perfect to take as a snack or to dip in vegetable sauces and pates.

7. **Cold pasta with dressing:** cook short pasta, like elbows, bows or sharks - the one that best fits your baby's grip and safety - drain well and dress with a drizzle of olive oil, halved cherry tomatoes, fresh cheese cubes, chopped herbs and a pinch of oregano or basil. Store it in a container and take it on a picnic or to the beach for a complete and refreshing lunch.

As you can see, the possibilities are endless and only limited by your imagination and your favorite ingredients. The key is to always include a source of carbohydrates (bread, tortillas, pasta, rice...), a protein (meat, fish, egg, legumes, dairy...) and one or two vegetables or fruits. And don't forget to also bring water or healthy drinks to maintain hydration, especially in the hot months.

Another advantage of these recipes is that they usually appeal to the whole family, so you won't have to make double preparations. And if you prepare them in mini format or individual portions, they will be perfect both for the baby's snack or lunch, as well as to take to work or include in the school lunchbox of older siblings. Win-win! I know you're looking forward to getting to the recipe chapter, where I've selected a variety.

## Addressing Criticism and Stares with Grace

As convinced as we are of the benefits of BLW and as much as we enjoy it at home, it is normal to feel a little more self-conscious or insecure when we practice it in public. After all, BLW is still not the social norm and can draw attention or arouse curiosity (and sometimes, mistrust) from others.

Whether it's a waiter looking at us strangely when we order a toast for our 6-month-old baby, grandparents insisting that "this way they won't eat anything", or parents asking us with concern if we are not afraid of choking... Sooner or later, we will have to deal with some comment or gesture that questions our feeding approach.

In those moments, it is easy to feel judged, questioned or even attacked in our parenting abilities. We may be overwhelmed by a mixture of anger, shame and the urge to justify ourselves or convince the other person that we are doing the right thing. But in reality, those reactions are usually more counterproductive than effective and only contribute to generating more tension and discomfort.

So, how can we handle those situations with grace and assertiveness, without losing our inner peace or our enjoyment of the moment? Here are some tips:

1. **Mentally anticipate and prepare:** Before leaving home, visualize some possible uncomfortable situations that could arise and think about how you would like to respond. Having a mental "script" of phrases and attitudes that make you feel comfortable and confident will help you react more calmly and confidently in the moment.

2. **Don't take the bait:** If someone makes a negative comment or a malicious question, take a deep breath and don't take it personally. Remember that most of the time, those criticisms stem from ignorance, fear or prejudice, not from ill intent. Instead of getting angry or defensive, try to respond with kindness and empathy.

3. **Use humor and lightness:** Sometimes, the best way to defuse a tense situation is with a smile and a witty response. For example, if someone tells you "this way they won't eat anything", you can reply something like "well, luckily they still breastfeed/bottle-feed, so they won't go hungry" or "yeah, we're teaching them to appreciate gourmet food, haha". Humor helps to relax the atmosphere and to take the edge off the matter.

4. **Offer brief and positive information:** If you notice that the other person has a genuine interest in understanding BLW, you can take the opportunity to share some relevant fact or benefit. For example "well, since they eat alone, they have developed a lot of motor skills" or "the truth is that we are delighted, they eat everything and really enjoy family meals". But don't get into long explanations or justifications, just share your experience in a natural and positive way.

5. **Establish boundaries with firmness and respect:** If despite your conciliatory attitude, the other person insists on criticizing or questioning your decisions, don't be afraid to set a clear and respectful boundary. Something like "I appreciate your concern, but we have studied the subject a lot and are very happy with how we are doing things. We respect that others do it differently, but for us this is the best option". Don't engage in debates or justify yourself further, simply reaffirm your position and change the subject.

6. **Focus on your baby and your family:** In the end, what matters is that you feel comfortable and confident with your way of feeding. Outside opinions are just that - opinions - and they don't have to make you doubt your abilities. So, in those moments, try to abstract yourself from other people's looks or comments and focus on enjoying the present moment with your baby and the people with whom you have chosen to share a table and tablecloth.

7. **Find your community and surround yourself with support:** Having other families nearby who also practice BLW can be a great relief and a source of mutual understanding.

Remember, each family has the right to make the parenting decisions they consider most appropriate for their children, always from a place of respect, love and responsibility. BLW is just one more option, as valid and beneficial as others, and it doesn't have to please or convince everyone. The goal is not to change society's mentality or become standard bearers for BLW, but simply to enjoy the experience of accompanying your baby in their discovery of autonomous, healthy and pleasurable eating.

Keep sharing those unique and unrepeatable moments around the table with them, full of laughter, stains, bits on the floor and unconditional love. Because that is what the baby will remember and treasure in their heart when they are older. Not a spotless baby who ate like a miniature adult, but a happy, curious and loved one, who learned to enjoy food as a shared family adventure. And that is priceless and does not depend on the approval of anyone but yourselves. Without fears or comparisons. Celebrating your baby's individuality and the wisdom of your instinct. And savoring each shared moment, however chaotic or imperfect it may be.

Because those moments, so everyday and yet so magical, are the ones that weave the unique and special bond between your baby and you. And that is worth more than all the guides and advice in the world. Thank you for letting me accompany you on this adventure. It has been a pleasure and an honor. But now it's up to you to continue writing your own story, with love, confidence and a lot of sense of humor. Bon appetit!

## Key points

o *With a little planning, flexibility and sense of humor, it is possible to enjoy and practice BLW away from home, whether in restaurants, friends' homes or while traveling.*

o *When eating in restaurants, choose family-friendly places, ask for simple adaptations to the menu, bring some foods and utensils from home, choose a good "timing" and be realistic with your expectations.*

o *Prepare a good repertoire of portable and easy-to-prepare BLW meals, such as sandwiches, skewers, omelets, mini meatballs or pasta salads. Variety and creativity are key!*

o *To handle possible criticism or uncomfortable looks, mentally anticipate, respond with humor and assertiveness, offer brief and positive information, set boundaries if necessary and focus on enjoying the moment with your family.*

o *Remember that BLW is a valid and beneficial option, but it doesn't have to please everyone. Trust your judgment, seek support and don't let outside opinions cloud the experience of accompanying your baby in their eating.*

# RECIPES

Dairy-free

Gluten-free

Egg-free

# Chapter 10: Recipes

1. Microwave Baked Apple
2. Oat-Banana Delight
3. Berry Breakfast
4. Hummus
5. Sailor Muffin
6. Juicy Chicken Waffles
7. Nutritious Turkey Burger
8. Broccoli Nuggets
9. Lentil Pasta with Avocado Sauce
10. Zucchini Meat Rolls
11. Healthy Fajitas
12. Guacamole
13. Three Delights Rice
14. Salty Crackers
15. Spinach Crepes
16. Beet Pate
17. Quesadillas
18. Yogurt and Mango Ice Cream
19. Pumpkin Muffins

Infant Nook

# Microwave Baked Apple

**Free from:**

**Ingredients:**

- ✓ 1 apple (Fuji, Gala...)
- ✓ Cinnamon powder (optional)
- ✓ Water

**Preparation:**

1. Wash the apple, remove the core and seeds and cut into small pieces. The skin is optional.
2. Place the pieces in a microwave-safe container and add a splash of water to the bottom, just enough so they don't stick.
3. Cover the container, leaving an opening for steam to escape, and cook in the microwave at maximum power for 3-4 minutes. Check that it is tender by pricking with a fork. If not, put it in for one or two more minutes.
4. Remove carefully, let it temper a bit and mash slightly with a fork. Sprinkle with cinnamon if you want to give it a special touch.
5. Offer it to your baby and enjoy watching how they explore its smell, texture and taste!

**Note:**

An interesting variation would be to mix the apple with other fruits, such as pear, banana or blueberries, to vary flavors and textures. You can also add a teaspoon of cereals like oatmeal or millet, to give it more density and an original touch. The possibilities are endless, so experiment according to your baby's interest.

Infant Nook

# Oat-Banana Delight

**Free from:**

## Ingredients:

- ✓ Ripe banana
- ✓ 1 egg (or 1 tsp ground flax seeds with 3 tbsp water, for vegan option)
- ✓ 2 tbsp whole rolled oats
- ✓ 1 tbsp whole wheat flour
- ✓ Cinnamon to taste

## Preparation:

1. Mash the banana with a fork until pureed.
2. Beat the egg and mix it with the puree. If using the vegan substitute, incorporate it now.
3. Add the oats, flour and cinnamon. Mix well until you have a homogeneous batter.
4. Heat a non-stick skillet over medium heat and drop spoonfuls of the batter, leaving space between them. The smaller, the easier for your baby to grab.
5. Cook for about 2-3 minutes on each side or until golden brown. Watch that they don't burn.
6. Let them cool a bit before offering them whole to your baby. You can also cut them into strips if that works better.
7. Store leftover pancakes in a container in the fridge (2-3 days) or freeze them (up to 3 months). You can reheat them in the toaster or microwave.

**Note:**

As variations, you can substitute the banana for applesauce or pumpkin puree. Or add other flavors like vanilla, orange zest, ground nuts... You can even add a little natural peanut butter or jam for spreading. Doesn't it make your mouth water already? Your little one will love them!

# Berry Breakfast

**Free from:**

**Ingredients:**

- ✓ A handful of blueberries
- ✓ 1 large strawberry
- ✓ Orange peel
- ✓ Half a banana
- ✓ 2 tablespoons of oatmeal
- ✓ Cinnamon to taste

**Preparation:**

1. In a pot over low heat, place a cup of water, wait for it to boil, add the orange peel, the strawberry in small pieces and the handful of blueberries.
2. After 5 minutes, when a jam has formed, remove from heat and let cool.
3. Remove the orange peel, add a little more water and blend. Return the blended mixture to the pot and add the oatmeal and stir until the desired texture is achieved.
4. Once the desired texture is achieved, add the mashed banana.

Note: you can add any red fruit. The photo presentation is designed to visually highlight the ingredients, but remember, as we have learned throughout the book, not to present the cuts in this way.

**Note:**

You can vary the recipe using other seasonal fruits, such as peaches, apricots, apple or pear. Or add other healthy toppings like chopped nuts, ground chia or flax seeds, or even a splash of plant-based milk (after one year). Each bowl will be an adventure of flavors and textures!

# Hummus

**Free from:**

**Ingredients:**

- ✓ 1 cup of soaked chickpeas for 12h (put in a container with double the amount of water) or already cooked chickpeas (if using canned, make sure they don't have additives)
- ✓ Lemon juice (to taste)
- ✓ 1 garlic clove (optional)
- ✓ 1 tablespoon of tahini (optional)
- ✓ Extra virgin olive oil

**Preparation:**

5. If using soaked chickpeas: place 2 fingers of water and lightly cook the chickpeas (after soaking them) until they are soft.
6. If the chickpeas are already cooked: blend all the ingredients until they form a paste.

Note: It can be offered spread on bread, or as a dip for cooked and soft vegetables (thin strips of carrot, pepper, sweet potato, potato, eggplant).

**Note:**

You can make the hummus thicker or thinner by adding more or less water or oil, depending on the desired consistency. You can also flavor it with spices like cumin, paprika or turmeric, or even add other vegetables, like roasted pepper or cooked beets. A rainbow of possibilities for your baby's senses!

# Sailor Muffin

**Free from:**

**Ingredients:**

- ✓ 2 eggs
- ✓ 3 tablespoons of cooked flaked fish (can be either oily or white fish)
- ✓ Olive oil and spices to taste (garlic, lemon, rosemary, thyme

**Preparation:**

1. Brown the garlic in oil.
2. Add the flaked fish and the spices you want to add, sauté for a few minutes.
3. Mix the eggs with the fish, and place in the molds.
4. If desired, sprinkle with breadcrumbs (contains gluten) on top and bake for 15 minutes in a preheated oven at 200ºC.

Note: You can keep them for up to 24 hours in the fridge, but it is better to consume them right away.

**Note:**

You can use any type of fish you like or have on hand, whether fresh, frozen or canned (in water or olive oil). If opting for the latter, remember to drain it well and check that it has no added salt. Some good options are salmon, hake, sole, sea bass or tuna.

If you want to give them a crunchy touch and extra fiber, you can coat them in whole wheat breadcrumbs or crushed oatmeal before baking. Or serve them with a light yogurt and grated cucumber sauce. Endless combinations to expand your little gourmet's palate!

# Juicy Chicken Waffles

**Free from:**

### Ingredients:

- ✓ 1 chicken breast
- ✓ 3 tablespoons of whole wheat flour
- ✓ 1 cup of raw zucchini
- ✓ 2 tablespoons of crushed tomato
- ✓ 1 egg / 1 tablespoon of flax seeds and 3 of water)
- ✓ Oregano to taste
- ✓ Cheese (after one year)

Infant Nook

## Preparation:

5. Cut and cook the chicken until well done.
6. Add all the ingredients to a food processor and blend.
7. Grease the waffle iron with a little olive oil and pour in the batter and cook.

Note: They can be made in the oven with a silicone mold, for about 15-20 minutes at 180ºC. Or in the air-fryer for 10 minutes at 180ºC.

**Note:**

To make these waffles 100% vegetable, you can replace the egg with ground flax seeds mixed with water, which act as a binder and provide omega-3 fatty acids and lignans with beneficial anti-inflammatory and hormonal effects. If your baby is already one year old and tolerates milk protein well, you can sprinkle a little grated cheese on top to gratin, or accompany with a light bechamel sauce. Another option is to make a waffle sandwich filled with mashed avocado, tomato and shredded chicken. A flavor explosion in every bite!

# Nutritious Turkey Burger

Free from:

## Ingredients:

- ✓ 500 g of minced turkey meat
- ✓ 200 g of grated zucchini
- ✓ 1 grated carrot (you can use other vegetables or add new ones)
- ✓ 1 egg (can be substituted by 1 tbsp of chickpea flour)
- ✓ ¼ onion
- ✓ 1 garlic clove
- ✓ Spices

## Preparation:

1. Chop the 500g of turkey meat, mix the already minced meat with the grated zucchini and carrot (important to drain them before mixing).
2. Peel the onion and garlic clove, chop or grate them and add them to the previous mixture.
3. Beat the egg and add it, mixing it well with the rest of the ingredients.
4. Add the spices we want (for example, ground pepper, ground cumin).
5. Mix everything well, add a tablespoon of breadcrumbs to give a greater consistency.
6. Give the shape we want to the burgers depending on the age of your baby.
7. We can make them in the pan with a drizzle of oil until golden or in the previously hot oven, about 7 minutes at 200ºC.

Note: You can keep them cooked in the freezer for about 3 months.

**Note:**

If desired, you can make them in an elongated finger shape or mini-balls for an even more fun and manageable presentation.

You can accompany them with slices of avocado, tomato and cucumber, or with a natural yogurt and fresh herb sauce. Or even assemble mini-burgers with toasted whole-wheat bread and tender lettuce. A complete and balanced feast in a single bite!

# Broccoli Nuggets

**Free from:**

### Ingredients:

- ✓ 2 medium potatoes
- ✓ 1 head of broccoli
- 1 egg (optional)
- ✓ Breadcrumbs (optional)
- ✓ Extra virgin olive oil
- ✓ Nutmeg (optional)

### Preparation:

1. Cook the potatoes in a pot until they are soft, take them out and mash them with a fork.
2. Steam the broccoli until tender and mix well with the potatoes, add a tablespoon of olive oil and nutmeg (to taste). Here you can add the egg and breadcrumbs, mix well until you get a uniform dough.
3. Make balls with the dough and shape them into nuggets, place them on an oven tray with baking paper. Bake at 200ºC on both sides for 10-15 minutes until golden brown.

Note: They can be kept in the fridge for 3-4 days in an airtight container.

**Note:**

These vegetable nuggets are a much healthier and more nutritious version than the classic fried chicken ones. Being made mainly of broccoli and potato, they provide a great variety of vitamins, minerals, fiber and antioxidants, with hardly any saturated fats or additives. Broccoli is an exceptional cruciferous vegetable, rich in vitamin C, vitamin K, folates, calcium and sulfurous compounds with powerful anticancer properties. Thanks to its soft texture and flavor, it is very well accepted by babies.

These nuggets are perfect as a light dinner or to take as a snack to the park. You can serve them with a homemade tomato sauce, with beet or carrot ketchup, or with a guacamole or hummus dip. They are also delicious accompanied by baked sweet potato wedges or a quinoa and vegetable salad. A rainbow of possibilities to enjoy eating healthy!

From 9 months

# Lentil Pasta with Avocado Sauce

Free from:

**Ingredients:**

- ✓ Lentil pasta
- ✓ 2 ripe avocados
- ✓ 2 hard-boiled eggs
- ✓ 15 g EVOO
- ✓ 1 splash of water

**Preparation:**

1. Cook the pasta following the instructions on the package.
2. For the sauce: Blend all the ingredients and add to the cooked pasta.

**Note:**

This recipe is very versatile and can be adapted according to the tastes and needs of each family. For example, whole-wheat pasta can be used instead of lentil pasta, mild spices such as oregano or cumin can be added, or the sauce can be enriched with a little natural yogurt or low-salt fresh cheese (after one year). It can also be served with strips of roasted bell pepper or with whole-wheat breadsticks for dipping. A healthy delight on a single plate!

# Zucchini Meat Rolls

**Free from:**

**Ingredients:**

- ✓ 2 sliced zucchini
- ✓ 500 g minced meat (chicken/turkey/veal/pork)
- ✓ 1 chopped onion
- ✓ 2 garlic cloves
- ✓ 250 g of natural tomato sauce
- ✓ Oregano
- ✓ Pepper
- ✓ 1 cup of water
- ✓ Grated cheese (after one year)
- ✓ Extra virgin olive oil

**Preparation:**

1. We start by preparing the filling. Sauté the onion and garlic with a little oil over low heat. When the onion starts to be transparent, add the minced meat (you can mince it yourself with a food processor), the tomato sauce and the cup of water.
2. We add the oregano, pepper and spices to taste, and cook until the meat is well done, then let it rest.
3. Meanwhile, we cut two zucchini into slices and bake them for about 9 minutes at 200ºC.
4. With the filling and the slices, we get to work. We fill the zucchini slices with the filling, and we roll the slice, leaving the mixture inside. We repeat the process with all the zucchini.
5. With the oven pre-heated to 200ºC, we bake for 10/15 minutes, and take it out when we see that it is golden brown.

Note: It is advisable to cut the rolls into slices to make it easier for the baby to pick them up with a fork

**Note:**

To serve the rolls, it is best to cut them into bite-size slices, so that the baby can easily pick them up with their hands and bring them to their mouth. They can be accompanied with other steamed or baked vegetables, such as baby carrots, broccoli or potato, or with a side of brown rice or quinoa. A complete and balanced dish to enjoy as a family!

# Healthy Fajitas

**Free from:**

## Ingredients:

- ✓ 2 chicken breasts in strips
- ✓ 1 diced sweet onion
- ✓ 1 red pepper in sticks
- ✓ 1 green pepper in sticks
- ✓ 2 tablespoons of EVOO
- ✓ Black pepper to taste
- ✓ Corn tortillas
- ✓ Guacamole (recipe below)

**Marinade:**
- ✓ 2 tablespoons of lemon juice
- ✓ 1 tablespoon of EVOO
- ✓ 1 chopped garlic clove

Infant Nook

## Preparation:

1. Cut the breasts into strips.
2. In a plate, mix all the marinade ingredients together with the breast, and let it rest for about 30 minutes in the fridge.
3. Heat oil in a pan and add the onion and peppers, cook until the onion is soft, about 8-10 minutes over medium-high heat. Add the chicken without the marinade to the very hot pan and cook until well done. Add the already cooked vegetables and mix everything well.
4. Heat the tortillas, you can do it in the microwave, for about 30 seconds, in the pan or in the oven. Serve with guacamole.

**Note:**

Roasted peppers can be substituted or combined with other vegetables such as zucchini, broccoli, carrot or corn.

To serve the fajitas safely and attractively for the baby, it is best to cut the tortillas into triangles or strips, and offer them together with the chopped vegetables and chicken on a wide plate or tray. The baby will be able to pick up the different elements with their hands, combining them to their liking, practicing the pincer grasp and chewing. A fun way to explore new flavors and textures as a family.

# Guacamole

**Free from:**

**Ingredients:**

✓ 1 ripe avocado

✓ ½ lemon or lime

✓ 1 ripe tomato

✓ ½ onion

Infant Nook

**Preparation:**

1. Cut the avocado in half, remove the pit and extract the avocado with the help of a spoon and put it in a bowl.
2. In the bowl, mash the avocado with a fork until it becomes a puree. Add the juice of half a lemon or lime to prevent the avocado from oxidizing and stir well so that it mixes with all the avocado puree.
3. Grate the tomato and incorporate it into the mixture and chop the onion into very small squares and incorporate it into the mixture.
4. Mix everything until it becomes a homogeneous mixture.

**Note:**

Guacamole is the perfect topping for fajitas, as it complements the nutritional contribution with healthy fats, fiber, vitamin K, folic acid and minerals such as potassium and magnesium. In addition, its creamy texture and mild flavor make it ideal for spreading or dipping pieces of tortilla or fajita.

Infant Nook

# Three Delights Rice

Free from:

## Ingredients:

- ✓ ½ glass of white rice
- ✓ ½ carrot
- ✓ 1 small handful of frozen peas
- ✓ 1 slice of cooked ham without salt
- ✓ 1 egg
- ✓ 2 glasses of water
- ✓ 1 tablespoon of EVOO1

## Preparation:

1. Put a pot of water to heat.
2. Peel and cut the carrot into small pieces.
3. When the water starts to boil, lower the heat and add both the chopped carrot and the ½ glass of rice.
4. After 10 minutes add the peas (in this case frozen), and cook for about 5 more minutes until the rice has absorbed all the cooking water. (If the rice is already cooked and there is water left over, it can be strained).
5. Next, cut the slice of cooked ham into small pieces and mix together with the rest in a bowl.
6. Finally, with the egg we make an omelet, making sure it is well cooked. We cut it into small pieces and add it to the bowl with the rest of the ingredients, mixing it well.

**Note:**

It can be served warm and chopped, for the baby to eat with their hands or practice with utensils. It admits many variations, such as adding shrimp or prawns, roasted peppers, seeds or soy sauce without salt, and it is ideal for sharing with the whole family. In addition, it can be prepared in quantity and frozen in individual portions.

Are you encouraged to try it at home? Surely your little adventurer will love this gastronomic journey through the Far East. Enjoy your meal!

# Salty Crackers

**Free from:**

Infant Nook

## Ingredients:

- ✓ 80 g of whole-oat flour
- ✓ ½ teaspoon of baking powder
- ✓ 1 tablespoon of EVOO
- ✓ 3 tablespoons of water
- ✓ Oregano
- ✓ Garlic powder
- ✓ Parsley

## Preparation:

1. Mix the water with the tablespoon of EVOO in a bowl.
2. In another bowl, mix the whole oat flour, baking powder and spices in a bowl, sift it with a strainer over the water and oil mixture.
3. Knead well until you have a moldable dough.
4. Let the dough rest in the bowl, covering the bowl with a cloth, for about 15 minutes.
5. Sprinkle flour on the work surface, and knead the dough until you get a thin dough, and have the shape you want for our cookies: you can help yourself with a mold.
6. Bake them for about 12 minutes at 180ºC.

Note:
- If the dough is too liquid, add more flour until you get a manageable consistency: if it is too thick, add more water.
- They can be kept in a closed container for 3-4 days in the fridge or 3 months in the freezer.

**Note:**

These homemade salty crackers are a nutritious and tasty alternative to commercial ones, perfect to accompany purees, creams or spreads in BLW. They are made with whole-oat flour, which provides complex carbohydrates, soluble fiber, B vitamins and minerals such as iron and magnesium; extra virgin olive oil, rich in monounsaturated fats and antioxidants; and aromatic spices and herbs such as oregano, garlic and parsley, which enhance the flavor without the need to add salt. The yeast helps to lighten the dough and facilitate digestion. Their crunchy texture and small size make them easy to pick up, bite and chew for the baby, promoting manual coordination and the development of oral musculature.

In addition, they can be kept in an airtight container for several days or frozen for months, to always have a healthy option on hand. They also admit variations such as adding seeds, grated cheese or sundried tomato.

# Spinach Crepes

### Ingredients:

- ✓ 2 eggs
- ✓ 120 g of whole-wheat flour
- ✓ 220 ml of whole milk
- ✓ 1 dessert spoon of EVOO
- ✓ 2 handfuls of fresh spinach

## Preparation:

1. Blend all the ingredients until a homogeneous batter is obtained.
2. Put a few drops of EVOO in a pan and pour part of the mixture. I recommend putting it on medium heat.
3. When little bubbles start to come out, carefully turn it over so that it browns on the other side.
4. Repeat the process until all the batter is used up.

Note: The crepes can be filled, for example, with tomato, cheese, avocado, cooked ham.

**Note:**

They can be served whole or cut, as a snack or light dinner, alone or filled with fresh cheese, avocado or other complementary ingredients. They are a complete and safe alternative to other iron-rich foods, perfect for BLW from one year on.

# Beet Pate

Free from:

### Ingredients:

- ✓ ½ cup cooked beet
- ✓ 200 g cooked chickpeas (or ½ can of cooked chickpeas without salt or additives and drained)
- ✓ 2 tablespoons of extra virgin olive oil
- ✓ 1 small garlic clove (optional)

Infant Nook

## Preparation:

1. Add all ingredients to the food processor and blend.
2. Serve immediately

## Note:

- It can be spread on bread or used for dipping, for example, sticks of cooked vegetables.
- It can be kept for up to 3 days in the fridge.

## Note:

This vegetable pate is an original and healthy option for spreading on bread or dipping with vegetable sticks in BLW from 12 months on.

It is advisable to prepare it in small quantities and consume it in 2-3 days, keeping it in the fridge in an airtight container, or freezing it in individual portions.

Infant Nook

# Quesadillas

**Free from:**

**Ingredients:**

- ✓ Corn or whole-wheat tortillas (preferably low in sodium)
- ✓ Grated cheese, low in fat and with no added salt
- ✓ Soft and finely chopped vegetables (such as spinach, zucchini or avocado)

**Preparation:**

1. Heat a non-stick skillet over medium heat.
2. Place a tortilla on the hot skillet.
3. Sprinkle a thin layer of grated cheese on half of the tortilla.
4. Add the chopped vegetables on top of the cheese.
5. Fold the tortilla in half, covering the filling.
6. Cook the quesadilla for a few minutes on each side, until the cheese melts and the tortilla is lightly golden.
7. Remove the quesadilla from the heat and let it cool slightly.
8. Cut it into small pieces or thin strips, suitable for your baby's small hands.
9. Serve them warm as a delicious and nutritious lunch or snack for your baby.

Note: Always make sure the vegetables are well cooked and cut into very small pieces to avoid choking hazards. In addition, you can customize the quesadillas with other healthy ingredients that your baby enjoys, such as shredded chicken or mashed black beans.

## Note:

They can be served warm, cut into small pieces or strips, and accompanied by sauces such as yogurt or guacamole for dipping. They admit many variations according to the available ingredients and family tastes.

# Yogurt and Mango Ice Cream

**Free from:**

**Ingredients:**

- ✓ **Unsweetened plain yogurt**
- ✓ **Mango**

Preparation:

1. Chop the mango and mix it well with the yogurt. The amount of yogurt depends on the molds you use.
2. Put the mixture in the ice cream molds and freeze for at least 3 hours.

Note: It can be made with any fruit.

**Note:**

It can be offered to the baby whole or cut, for them to suck and bite or eat with a spoon. It admits many variations of fruits and healthy toppings.

# Pumpkin Muffins

**Free from:**

## Ingredients:

- ✓ 240 g of roasted pumpkin
- ✓ 150 g of hydrated dates
- ✓ 40 g of 100% cocoa
- ✓ 70 g of whole oat flour
- ✓ 40 g of EVOO
- ✓ 4 eggs
- ✓ 15 g of yeast
- ✓ 100 g of dark chocolate >70% (optional)

Infant Nook

## Preparation:

1. Cook the pumpkin. You can do it in the microwave, peeling it and cutting it into small pieces, cover it with a microwave-safe transparent film, and cook it for about 13 minutes at maximum power. Prick it with a fork to make sure it is soft and cooked.
2. When it finishes, let it rest for about 2 minutes. Be careful not to burn yourself when uncovering it.
3. Put all the ingredients in a bowl and blend them, except for the chocolate.
4. Put half in the molds, add half of the dark chocolate in pieces, and add the other half of the batter.
5. On top of all the batter in the molds, add the other half of the dark chocolate in pieces.
6. Bake for about 20 minutes at 180ºC.

Storage: they last about 2-3 days in the fridge and about 3 months in the freezer.

**Note:**

These pumpkin and chocolate muffins are a special, nutritious and delicious snack or dessert option for BLW from 12 months on.

When baking the mixture in molds, a fluffy and juicy texture is achieved, with an intense aroma of pumpkin and chocolate. They can be served whole or split, warm or at room temperature, depending on the baby's skill. They keep for 2-3 days in the fridge or up to 3 months in the freezer.

They admit variations such as substituting the pumpkin for sweet potato or carrot, using other flours or adding spices and nuts.

# CONCLUSION

## Embracing the BLW Journey with Confidence and Joy

### *Dear mother or father,*

If you have made it this far, I can only tell you one thing: congratulations. Congratulations for having chosen to accompany your baby on this exciting and revolutionary journey that is Baby-Led Weaning. Congratulations for daring to question established opinions and seek a more respectful, natural feeding adapted to the needs of your little one. And congratulations for all the love, patience and dedication you have put into each page of this book and each step of this path.

I know it has not been easy. That there have been moments of doubts, fears, frustrations. That you have faced criticism, looks of misunderstanding, sleepless nights reading and consulting to make the best decision for your baby. And that sometimes, you have even felt that you were not doing enough or the right thing, because your little one did not eat as much as the neighbor's or because they continued to prefer certain textures over others.

But I want you to know that all of that is normal and does not define you as a mother or father. That there is no perfect BLW or a baby who does everything "by the book". That each family is a world and that the important thing is to find the balance and confidence in your own style of doing things. And that, above all, you have been offering your baby much more than solid foods. You have been giving them an invaluable treasure: your presence, your respect and your unconditional love.

Because BLW, in essence, is much more than a complementary feeding method. It is a way of understanding parenting and the relationship with our children from a deep respect for their individuality, their autonomy and their innate capacity for self-regulation. It is an invitation to trust the process, the natural development of their abilities and their insatiable curiosity to discover the world through all the senses.

By betting on BLW, you have given your baby the opportunity to explore foods at their own pace, without haste or pressure. You have allowed them to decide what, how much and at what speed they wanted to eat at each moment, respecting their cues of hunger and satiety. You have encouraged them to manipulate, smell, lick, bite and savor each little piece of food, enjoying the pleasure of textures and flavors beyond mere caloric intake. And you have integrated them from day one into your family meals and routines, making them feel an important and active part of that daily ritual so intimate and meaningful.

Thus, you have helped them develop crucial skills for their life, not only on a motor or nutritional level, but above all on an emotional and social level. You have conveyed to them that you trust their abilities, that you value their initiative and that you celebrate their achievements. You have taught them to listen to their own body, to enjoy without fear and to make autonomous decisions from love and respect for themselves. And you have given them indelible memories of laughter, games, culinary adventures as a family that will continue to nourish your bond beyond childhood.

For all this and much more, I thank you. Thank you for having trusted in this book as a guide and companion on your BLW journey. Thank you for having read it with an open mind and a curious heart, adapting each piece of advice and each idea to your unique and unrepeatable reality.

And thank you for continuing to bet every day on seeing your little one's feeding as a precious opportunity to sow health, but above all love and trust.

I hope these pages have served as inspiration, support and a hug in moments of doubt. I hope they have made you feel accompanied and understood, knowing that there are many other families out there living experiences similar to yours. And I hope they have given you wings to continue flying on this BLW journey with the certainty that you are doing great, simply because you are doing it with all the love in the world.

But remember that this is not the end of the journey, but only the beginning. That from now on an infinite universe of possibilities opens up before you to continue accompanying your little one in their relationship with food and with life. That each stage will bring you new challenges, new learnings and new joys to face together as a family. And that you are not alone on this path, but that you have an immense community of professionals, friends and parents and mothers who, like you, have chosen the path of respect, love and trust.

So keep going with that curious look and that smile on your face. Keep experimenting in the kitchen and at the table without fears or prejudices. Keep celebrating each little victory, each new food tried, each gesture of autonomy and satisfaction from your little one. And, above all, keep enjoying with them those magical and unrepeatable moments around a shared plate, a complicit laugh, a "mmmm" of pure delight.

Because this is your story and your path, and it does not resemble anyone else's. Because there is no infallible manual or single recipe for parenting, only the infinite love you put into it every day. And because, no matter what happens, the imprint you are leaving on your little one's heart is much deeper and more lasting than any stain on the tablecloth.

Thank you again for having let me be a witness and accomplice of your journey. It has been a gift and a constant learning that has filled me with hope and inspiration to continue accompanying other families on this exciting path. I hope we continue to meet on social media, in bookstores or in parks, to continue sharing our experiences, our doubts and our joys. Because, in the end, this is not about methods or labels, but about weaving a network of support and love that sustains and nourishes us all.

In the meantime, I wish you all the best on your BLW journey and beyond. May you continue to grow as a person and as a family, embracing challenges with enthusiasm and confidence. May you continue to fill your home and your life with good food, shared laughter and unforgettable moments. And may you, above all, continue to look at your little one with those eyes of wonder and pride, knowing that they are your best gift and your greatest achievement.

Thank you, bon appétit and see you soon!

With love,

*Amelia Benet*

# RESOURCES FOR FURTHER READING:

1. **American Academy of Pediatrics (AAP). (2021). "Feeding and Introducing Solid Foods During Breastfeeding." Available at:** https://www.healthychildren.org/English/ages-stages/baby/breastfeeding/Pages/Working-Together-Breastfeeding-and-Solid-Foods.aspx

2. **Perkin, M. R., Logan, K., Marrs, T., Radulovic, S., Craven, J., Flohr, C.,... & Lack, G. (2016). Randomized trial of introduction of allergenic foods in breast-fed infants. New England Journal of Medicine, 374(18), 1733-1743. Retrieved from** https://www.nejm.org/doi/full/10.1056/NEJMoa1514210

3. **Nwaru, B. I., Takkinen, H. M., Niemelä, O., Kaila, M., Erkkola, M., Ahonen, S., ... & Virtanen, S. M. (2014). Timing of infant feeding in relation to childhood asthma and allergic diseases. Journal of Allergy and Clinical Immunology, 134(2), 336-344. Retrieved from** https://www.jacionline.org/article/S0091-6749(14)00182-3/fulltext

4. **American Academy of Pediatrics (AAP). (2021). "When, What, and How to Introduce Solid Foods." Available at:** https://www.healthychildren.org/English/ages-stages/baby/feeding-nutrition/Pages/Switching-To-Solid-Foods.aspx

5. **Anales de Pediatría. (2011).** *Importance of iron deficiency in young children. Retrieved from* https://www.analesdepediatria.org/es-importancia-ferropenia-el-nino-pequeno-articulo-S1695403311000907

6.  Spanish Association of Pediatrics. (2018). *Recommendations on complementary feeding.* Retrieved from https://www.aeped.es/sites/default/files/documentos/recome ndaciones_aep_sobre_alimentacio_n_complementaria_nov20 18_v3_final.pdf

7.  American Academy of Pediatrics (AAP). (2021). "Starting Solid Foods." https://www.healthychildren.org/English/ages-stages/baby/feeding-nutrition/Pages/Starting-Solid-Foods.aspx

8.  American Academy of Pediatrics (AAP). (2021). "Food Allergy Reactions." https://www.healthychildren.org/English/ages-stages/baby/feeding-nutrition/Pages/Food-Allergy-Reactions.aspx

9.  American Academy of Pediatrics. (2012). *Breastfeeding and the use of human milk.* Pediatrics, 129(3), e827-e841. Recuperado de https://publications.aap.org/pediatrics/article/129/3/e827/3102 8/Breastfeeding-and-the-Use-of-Human-Milk

10. Spanish Association of Pediatrics. (2017). Breastfeeding, the best start for both. Retrieved from https://www.aeped.es/sites/default/files/201701-lactancia-materna-mejor-ambos.pdf

11. Forestell, C. A. (2017). Flavor perception and preference development in human infants. Annals of Nutrition and Metabolism, 70(Suppl. 3), 17-25. Retrieved from https://karger.com/anm/article/70/Suppl.%203/17/42393